1890 Special Census of the Civil War Veterans of the State of Maryland

Volume VII

Baltimore County and Baltimore City Institutions

L. Tilden Moore

HERITAGE BOOKS
2012

HERITAGE BOOKS
AN IMPRINT OF HERITAGE BOOKS, INC.

Books, CDs, and more—Worldwide

For our listing of thousands of titles see our website
at
www.HeritageBooks.com

Published 2012 by
HERITAGE BOOKS, INC.
Publishing Division
100 Railroad Ave. #104
Westminster, Maryland 21157

Copyright © 2005 L. Tilden Moore

Other Heritage Books by the author:

1890 Special Census of the Civil War Veterans of the State of Maryland:
Volume I, Garrett, Allegany and Washington Counties

Volume II, Carroll, Frederick, Montgomery, Prince George's, Calvert, Charles and St. Mary's Counties

Volume III, Howard, Anne Arundel, Harford, Cecil and Kent Counties and the United States Naval Academy

Volume IV, Caroline, Dorchester, Queen Anne's, Somerset, Talbot, Wicomico, and Worcester

Volume V, Baltimore City

Volume VII, Baltimore County and Baltimore City Institutions

———

Abstracts of Marriages and Deaths ... in the Newspapers of Frederick and Montgomery Counties, Maryland, 1831–1840

Index to Administration Accounts of Frederick County, 1750–1816 (Maryland)

All rights reserved. No part of this book may be reproduced or transmitted in any form or by any means, electronic or mechanical, including photocopying, recording or by any information storage and retrieval system without written permission from the author, except for the inclusion of brief quotations in a review.

International Standard Book Numbers
Paperbound: 978-0-7884-3178-4
Clothbound: 978-0-7884-3414-3

ACKNOWLEDGMENTS

I want to especially thank my good friend Edwin Cole Bearss, Historian Emeritus of the National Park Service, for his "Foreword" in introducing this volume series. Edwin is not only a historian of the Civil War. He is a reputable authority on other military arms and events. Words cannot express how appreciative I am for his generosity. Others who have lent their talents and expertise of knowledge in deciphering handwriting, and are very special people as well, are Mr. Francis P. O'Neill, Mr. Henry Peden, Mr. Mike Musick, and Mr. Thomas Hollowak. They all have several books and publications to their credit. Henry Peden has assisted me in proof reading all seven (7) volumes of this Special Census. To him, I owe a great deal of thanks for all his time and his most generous assistance and attentiveness in the overseeing of each of these volumes as well.

Some of Henry Peden's publications consist of the following: *A Collection of Maryland Church Records; A Guide to Genealogical Research in Maryland; Marylanders to Carolina; Inhabitants of Kent County, Maryland 1637-1787; Maryland Deponents 1634-1799.*

Thomas Hollowak is the Archivist at the University of Baltimore Langsdale Library. Tom is a graduate, along with myself, from the University of Maryland of Baltimore County, where we received our B. A. in History. Thomas Hollowak also received his M.A. in History from the University of Maryland.

The following are just a few of Thomas Hollowak's publications, newspapers and books to his credit: *Polonia in the Press; Marriages & deaths in the Baltimore Sun from 1837-1850; Marriages & Death in the Baltimore Sun from 1851-1860; Baltimore Polish Language Newspaper & Historical & Genealogical Abstracts 1891-1925.*

Michael Musick, who is a close friend, just retired from the National Archives, where he worked and was responsible for the old Military and Civil Records for over 30 years. Michael tried his best to read and ascertain effectiveness, the names of the Confederate Soldiers that were crossed out on the census. Without his help and effortless, many of the names would still be unreadable. I do appreciate his time and expertise, as well as his skill and performance.

Francis P. O'Neill is the Senior Reference Librarian of the Maryland Historical Society, where he has worked for close to 24 years. Francis P. O'Neill is like my right-hand man, and my main source for which I relied upon for proofing this entire book. At the Society, Francis used the following sources to check the names acquired and relative to the census: *1880, & 1900 Baltimore Census; 1890 & 1891 Baltimore City Directories; The History and Roster of Maryland Volunteers War of 1861-1865; Dielman'Hayward Card Files.*" Francis is responsible for several books accredited to his name, and amongst them are: "*Indexes to the Newspapers of New Hampshire*". He has published one book on Baltimore called "*Index of Obituaries and Marriages in the Baltimore Sun 1871 - 1875.*

Lastly, I sincerely want to express my gratitude to John P. Angeletti, Jr., for his assistance and fortitude in helping me edit and prepare this book for publication.

I hope that the Genealogical Community and Family Researchers, along with the Civil War Researchers, find and discover, perhaps, new knowledge and awareness most beneficial in these Seven Volumes for their Historical Research.

PREFACE

For Volume VII, which includes Baltimore County & Baltimore City Institutions, there is a table of contents. You will notice that in Volume VII, on pages 6 - 9 and 48 - 49, the following example of "6-2, and June 4" signifies the date that the names are added to the schedule. If there are several names under the date, they were added, as well. On pages 50 - 51 you will see that the number "92" signifies the year that the person was added to the list.

In these volumes, as in any other book you read, you will find mistakes. As you read the Special Schedule, you will notice mistakes made by the Enumerators and Clerks. Confederate names were marked through leaving them unreadable. Other times the names were legible and even misspelled. In the late 1800's there was still a lot of illiteracy: if a person could not read or spell he would generally make an "X," or somebody would write his name according to how it sounded. Some of the mistakes the proofreaders may have made may have included based on oral pronunciation, interpreting the spelling, where vowels may look like consonants and vice a versa. People may say we have spelled the name incorrectly and should spell the names according to how they are spelled today. According to twenty-first century standard this may be true in practice however, we should not change the method the Enumerators and Clerks used to spell names of the nineteen century. We are only trying to interpret the spelling of the Enumerators and Clerks of the latter century. We know that as education improved the spelling of names became more formal. That is why the proofreaders did not change the names so they would be spelled like they are today.

You will notice the following symbols "√" means it is a duplicate of a name already on the schedule. The other symbol "*" means the name was added by the Clerk to fill out the page for certain districts. You will see a copy from the original schedule which was used by the proofreaders. This will give you an idea as to what the proofreaders had to work with.

NATIONAL ARCHIVES

The schedules for each State or Territory generally comprise one or more bundles, and the bundles, with few exceptions, are arranged alphabetically by name of State or Territory; they are numbered in sequence from 54 through 66, 68 through 71, 72 ½, and 73 through 198. Bundles 1 through 53, containing practically all of the schedules for the States Alabama through Kansas and approximately half of those for Kentucky, appear to have been misplaced or destroyed prior to the transfer of the remaining schedules to the National Archives. There are no bundles numbered 67 and 72. Within each State the schedules are arranged numerically by supervisors' districts, and thereunder alphabetically by name of county, with the exception of the bundle containing the schedules for Oklahoma and Indian Territories (Roll 76), which as arranged numerically by enumeration district.

The following tables list the various States and Territories, corresponding bundles numbers, and the roll numbers of this microcopy on which the schedules for each State or Territory have been photographed. Roll 104 contains schedules for United States Vessels and Connecticut, Delaware, Florida, Idaho, Illinois and Kansas.

State or Territory	Bundle Nos.	Rolls Nos.
Kentucky	54 - 57	1 - 3
Louisiana	58 - 61	4 - 5
Maine	62 - 63	6 - 7
Maryland	64 - 66	8 - 10
Massachusetts	68 - 71 72 ½	11 - 16
Michigan	73 - 78	17 - 21
Minnesota	79 - 82	22 - 25
Mississippi	83 - 86	26
Missouri	87 - 95	27 - 34
Montana	96	35
Nebraska	97 - 99	36 - 38
Nevada	100	39
New Hampshire	101	40
New Jersey	102 - 104	41 - 43
New Mexico	105	44
New York	106 - 118	45 - 57
North Carolina	119 - 123	58
North Dakota	124	59
Ohio	125 - 140	60 - 75
Oklahoma and Indian Territories	141	76
Oregon	142 - 143	77
Pennsylvania	144 - 158	78 - 91
Rhode Island	159	92
South Carolina	160 - 161	93
South Dakota	162 - 163	94
Tennessee	164 - 169	95 - 98
Texas	170 - 176	99 - 102
Utah	177	103

U. S. Vessels and Navy Yards	178	104
Vermont	179	105
Virginia	180 - 185	106 - 107
Washington	186 - 187	108
West Virginia	188 - 189	109 - 110
Wisconsin	190 - 195	111 - 116
Wyoming	196	117
Washington D. C. (Lincoln Post No. 3)	197	
Miscellaneous (California - Kansas)	198	118

(These schedules are a part of a body of records in the National Archives designated as Record Group No. 15, Records of the Veterans' Administration.

TABLE OF CONTENTS

Precinct 1st District Catonsville	p. 2
2nd Precinct 1st Dist. Ellicott City	p. 6
Wethendville	p. 9
2nd Dist. Powhatan	p. 10
1st Precinct 3rd District Mt. Washington	p. 17
Owing Mills	p. 22
14th District Glyndon	p. 24
Reisterstown	p. 27
Fifth District Mt. Carmel	p. 28
3rd District West of Fall Turnpike	p. 29
Sixth Election District Eklo	p. 30
Baltimore City	p. 35
S. ½ 2nd Precinct, 7th District Hereford	p. 38
1st Precinct 8th District Glencor	p. 43
Lutherville	p. 51
1st Prc. 9th Dist. Govanstown	p. 53
1st Precinct 10th Dist. Monkton	p. 64
1st Prec. 11 District Baldwin	p. 67
Highlandtown & Canton	p. 73
1st Prect. 12th District Clinton St.	p. 74
3rd Precinct 1st District Parkville	p. 81
4th Prect 12 District Fullerton	p. 82
Sparrows Point	p. 86
Mount Winas P. O.	p. 90
St. Mary's Industrial School	p. 94
2nd Pr. 13 E. District St. Dennis	p. 94
Bay View Asylum	p. 96
Baltimore	p. 100
Samuel Ready Asylum	p. 101
The U. S. Marine Hospital	p. 102
Hebrew Hospital & Asylum	p. 103
Notre Dame	p. 103
2nd District	p. 104
Baltimore City Jail	p. 104
Maryland General Hospital	p. 105 & 107
Fort McHenry	p. 106
Maryland Penitentiary	p. 107
St. Joseph's Hospital	p. 110

Eleventh Census of the United States.

SPECIAL SCHEDULE.
SURVIVING SOLDIERS, SAILORS, AND MARINES, AND WIDOWS, ETC.

Page No. _____
Supervisor's District No. 1
Enumeration District No. 433

Persons who served in the Army, Navy, and Marine Corps of the United States during the war of the rebellion (who are survivors), and widows of such persons, in 8 Dist 1st Precinct, County of Baltimore, State of Maryland, enumerated in June, 1890.

Chas. M. Chilcoat, Enumerator.

From Schedule No. 1 House No.	Family No.	Names of Surviving Soldiers, Sailors, and Marines, and Widows.	Rank.	Company.	Name of Regiment or Vessel.	Date of Enlistment.	Date of Discharge.	Length of Service. Yrs. Mos. Days.
24	25	Nancy Adams widow of Jacob Adams	Private	A	x x x	x x 186_	x x 186_	x x x
28	29	R. Darrett — Wilks	—	K	7 Md Inf	28 June 1863	2 July 1865	2 6 14
38	39	William H. Clark	Private	H	201 Pa Inf	20 Aug 1864	22 June 1865	10 21
45	46	Abraham Scott	Priv't	x	x x	x 1862	x x 1865	x x x
46	47	Charles Robuck	Private	—	—	— 186_	— 186_	— — —
55	56	John Robinson	Teamster	—	—	— 186_	— 186_	— — —
73	78	Samuel Colbert	Private	K	13 Md Inf	18 Sep 1861	18 Jan 1864	2 5
75	74	Samuel Colbert	Private	K	13 Md Inf	18 Sep 1861	18 Jan 1864	2 5
68	69	Joshua Ambrose	Private	D	8 Md Inf	30 Aug 1862	31 May 1865	2 7 1
84	87	William Tracy	Private	B	3 Md Inf	23 Mar 1865	28 July 1865	4 5
97	103	Benjamin Johnson	Private	D	28 US Vol	20 May 1864	8 Nov 1865	1 5 18
112	118	Lewis W. Goss	Private	F	Purnell Legion Md Inf	21 Oct 1861	24 Dec 1864	

	POST-OFFICE ADDRESS. 10	DISABILITY INCURRED. 11	REMARKS. 12
1	Cockeysville Balto Co Md	x	x
2	Cockeysville Balto Co Md	Head affected	At Petersburg Artillery Fire
3	Cockeysville Balto Co Md	Weak Back	
4	Cockeysville Balto Co Md	Hip out of Place	He has no papers
5	Cockeysville Balto Co Md		He has No papers
6	Cockeysville Balto Co Md		He has no papers
7	Cockeysville Balto Co Md	Heart Disease	Captured and exchanged
8	Cockeysville Balto Co Md	Heart Disease	Was reenlisted Said Book Ret
9	Cockeysville Balto Co Md	Rheumatism	x
10	Lutherville Baltimore Co Md		Objection made to Registration
11	Cockeysville Baltimore Co Md		
12	Bosley Baltimore Co		

1890 Special Census
of the Civil War Veterans of the State of Maryland

Volume # VII
BALTIMORE COUNTY
&
BALTIMORE CITY INSTITUTIONS

Page No. 1
Supervisor's District No. 1
Enumeration District No. 411

Eleventh Census of the United States

SPECIAL SCHEDULE
SURVIVING SOLDIERS, SAILORS, AND MARINES, AND WIDOWS, ETC.

Persons who served in the Army, Navy, and Marine Corps of the United States during the war of the rebellion (who are survivors), and widows of such persons, in   Precinct 1st District   County of   Baltimore
State of   Maryland.   enumerated in June 1890

Geo. G. Robinson
Enumerator

	1	2	3	4	5	6	7	8	9
									Yrs Mos Dys
15234.	√UNGER, Robt. D Catonsville, Balto., Co.			Sargeant Lost 3rd finger on left hand at Spottyslvania C. H. Wilderness fight	H	6 Md. Inf	Near June 1862	April 1864	2 years
15235.	WATTS, Joseph W. Catonsville, Balto., Co.			Private Scurvy in mouth, and also cannot use right arm at times	C	2 Md. Cav.	8 July 1863	6 Feb. 1864	0 6 28
15236.	WHEELER, John Catonsville, Balto., Co.			Private	C	2 Md. Cav.	8 July 1863	6 Feb. 1864	0 6 28
15237.	√WHEELER, John Catonsville, Balto., Co.			Private		Patapsco Guards Md.	21 Mar. 1864	17 Aug. 1865	0 5 26
15238.	Robt. D. Unger, alias UNDERWOOD, Robt. Catonsville, Balto., Co., Md.			Corporal	E	25 U. S. Inf.	18 Oct. 1864	19 Oct. 1867	3 0 1
15239.	YOUNG, Geo. W. Catonsville	34	34	Sailor		Cannot find ot his wife does not know, away from home	186	186	
15240.	Barbary Porter, widow of PORTER, John Catonsville, Balto., Co., Md.			Private	E	2 Md. Cav.	10 July 1863	31 Jan. 1864	0 6 21
15241.	BRADY, James Catonsville, Balto., Co., Md.			Drummer Discharge lost in flood	H	11 Md. Inf.	June 1865	Not known 186	
15242.	SHELDOLLAR, John Catonsville, Balto., Co., Md.			Corporal	A	Artillary Maryland Junior	23 June 1864	19 Jan. 1864	6 26
15243.	JAMES, Abel D. Catonsville, Balto., Co., Md.			Private		This man cannot tell about his enlistment is simple mined 5 Md. Inf.	186	186	
15244.	ROLLINS, Dorsey Catonsville, Balto., Co., Md.	80	81	Private This man is away from home I cannot find out any more	G	Cannot find out anything	186	186	

	1	2	3	4	5	6	7	8	9
15245.	Emily Henson, widow of HENSON, Wm. H. Catonsville, Balto., Co., Md.	123	126	Cannot find out anything was discharged on account of sickness and died before he got home				186	186

Special Schedule. Surviving Soldiers, Sailors, and Marines, and Widows, etc.

Page

S. D.: ; E. D.: ; Minor Civil Division.:

	1	2	3	4	5	6	7	8	9
									Yrs Mos Dys
15246.	TURNER, John Catonsville Balto., Co., Md.			Private	C	23 U. S. Inf.	June 1862	23 Dec. 1865 Cannot find out discharge papers lost	3 6
15247.	WATKINS, Benjamin Catonsville Balto., Co., Md.			Private Health is bad caused by service enlisted about August 1st after Battle of Petersburg, discharged papers lost	A	28 Ind. Inf.	186	186 Discharged Christmas after war in Indianapolis, suffering with cough and rheumatism while in service	
15248.	*UNGER, Robt. B. Catonsville, Md.	8	8				186	186	
15249.	*BURKE, John 1st District Balto., Co., Md.	191	193				186	186	
15250.	*FEAST, Mary J. 1st District Balto., Co., Md.	140	142	widow			186	186	

Page No. 1
Supervisor's District No. 1
Enumeration District No. 411

Eleventh Census of the United States

SPECIAL SCHEDULE
SURVIVING SOLDIERS, SAILORS, AND MARINES, AND WIDOWS, ETC.

Persons who served in the Army, Navy, and Marine Corps of the United States during the war of the rebellion (who are survivors), and widows of such persons, in 1st District Pct. County of Baltimore State of Maryland. enumerated in June 1890

Geo. G. Robinson
Enumerator

	1	2	3	4	5	6	7	8	9
									Yrs Mos Dys
15251.	Mary Henson, widow of HENSON, Jacob Catonsville Balto., Co., Md.			Cannot find out about him			186	186	
15252.	John Green alias BURK, John Catonsville Balto., Co., Md.			Private Discharge lost	F	2 D. C. Inf.	Sept. 1863	Jan. 1866	

Page -3-

Page No.
Supervisor's District No. 1
Enumeration District No. 412

Eleventh Census of the United States

SPECIAL SCHEDULE
SURVIVING SOLDIERS, SAILORS, AND MARINES, AND WIDOWS, ETC.

Persons who served in the Army, Navy, and Marine Corps of the United States during the war of the rebellion (who are survivors), and widows of such persons, in   1st District Balto. Co. MD.   County of   Baltimore
State of   Maryland.   enumerated in June 1890

James Wilson
Enumerator

	1	2	3	4	5	6	7	8	9 Yrs	Mos	Dys
15253.	BEWLEY, Isaac T. Catonsville Balto., Md.	5	9	Sergeant	C	2 Md. Cav.	6 June 1863	5 Feb. 1864	0	8	0
15254.	RYAN, William Catonsville Balto., Md.	134	141	Sergeant Prison - 4 months Bell Ile	F	12 Penn. Inf.	Mar. 1 1862	20 June 1865	3	4	20
15255.	SMITH, George W. Catonsville Balto., Md.	151	155	Private		2nd Ind. Bat.	5 Aug. 1862	8 July 1863	0	11	4
15256.	REED, Andrew M. Catonsville Balto., Md.	155	159	Sergeant	B	102 Penn. Inf.	18 Aug. 1861	3 July 1865	3	10	12
15257.	LAKE, Charles H. Catonsville Balto., Md.	170	175	Steward	U. S. A.		15 Apr. 1862	Aug. 1865	3	5	0
15258.	HOWARD, Cornelias H. Catonsville Balto., Md.	176	181	Private	E	1 Md. Inf.	10 May 1861	May 1864	3	0	0
15259.	√HOWARD, Cornelias H. Catonsville Balto., Md.	176	181	Musition Reenlisted for 3 yrs	F	1 Md. Inf.	May 1864	Apr. 1865	0	11	0
15260.	WOLF, John W. Catonsville Balto., Md.	75	78	Private	D	3 Md. Inf.	1864	1865			
15261.	DIXON, John F. Catonsville Balto., Md.	201	206	Private Feet frost frosted	G	9 Md. Inf.	26 June 1863	5 May 1864	0	10	20
15262.	BRADY, James W. Catonsville Balto., Md.						186	186			
15263.	LINDER, Edgar T. Catonsville Balto., Md.	336	339	Private	F	45 Ill. Inf.	17 Oct. 1861	29 May 1862	0	7	12
15264.	Reinlisted √LINDER, Edgar T. Catonsville Balto., Md.	336	339	Private	G	78 Penn. Inf.	25 Feb. 1865	11 Sep. 1865	0	6	17

Special Schedule. Surviving Soldiers, Sailors, and Marines, and Widows, etc.

Page

S. D.:   ; E. D.:   ; Minor Civil Division.:   1st Precinct

	1	2	3	4	5	6	7	8	9		
										Yrs	Mos Dys
15265.	BRILL, Henry	367	370	Private	A	1 Md. Inf.	May 1861	1863	2	0	0
15266.	*KUMMER, Arnold 1st Precinct of Baltimore, Md.	258	261				186	186			
15267.	*WYSHAM, William E. Catonsville Baltimore, Md.	116	116				186	186			
15268.	*BROWN, Richard A. Catonsville Baltimore, Md.	73	76				186	186			
15269.	*GREEN, Allen Catonsville Baltimore, Md.	71	74				186	186			

Page No. 1
Supervisor's District No. 1
Enumeration District No. 412-A

Eleventh Census of the United States

SPECIAL SCHEDULE
SURVIVING SOLDIERS, SAILORS, AND MARINES, AND WIDOWS, ETC.

Persons who served in the Army, Navy, and Marine Corps of the United States during the war of the rebellion (who are survivors), and widows of such persons, in   Catonsville   County of   Baltimore   ,
State of   Maryland.   enumerated in June 1890

Samuel J. Bell
Enumerator

	1	2	3	4	5	6	7	8	9	
									Yrs	Mos Dys
15270.	EVANS, Joseph T. Catonsville, Md.	11	11	Private	F	2 Md. Inf.	Mch 1864	Jan. 1865	0	10

Supplemental Report

Eleventh Census of the United States

Page No.
Supervisor's District No. 1
Enumeration District No. 413

SPECIAL SCHEDULE
SURVIVING SOLDIERS, SAILORS, AND MARINES, AND WIDOWS, ETC.

Persons who served in the Army, Navy, and Marine Corps of the United States during the war of the rebellion (who are survivors), and widows of such persons, in   2nd Precinct 1st Dist.   County of   Balto.   ,
State of   Maryland.   enumerated in June 1890

Chas. A. Herrmann
Enumerator

1	2	3	4	5	6	7	8	9
								Yrs Mos Dys

	No.	Name / Residence	Col 2	Col 3	Rank	Co.	Regiment	Enlisted	Discharged	Yrs	Mos	Dys	Notes
	15271.	TRUEHEART, Adolphus H. (Conf) / Ellicott City, Md.	2 / Bad health	2	Private	Young General	Wise brigade / 46 Va. Inf.	1862	186 / Transferred to Custom House				
	15272.	IGLEHART, John H. (Conf) / Ellicott City, M.	5 / General debility	5	Private	I	21 Tex. Inf.	May 1862	Sep. 1862 / Transferred to Medical Dept.	4 or 5			
	15273.	Orlando Boederson, alias / WALLIS, Jno. W. / Ellicott City, Md.	12	12	Private		Balto. Battery of Light Artillery / No 4 Gun	15 Aug. 1862	186	3			
3)	15274.	CAMPBELL, Geo. W. / Ellicott City, Md.	8	8	Private		5 Ohio Inf.	1 May 1864	28 Aug. 1864			120	
6-2)	15275.	HOSE, Solomon / Ellicott City, Md.	13	13	Seargeant	L	P. H. B. Cavalry Md.	24 Mch 1864	28 June 1865	1	3	4	
	15276.	CRAMBLETT, Joseph S. / Ellicott City, Md.	16	16	Private	B	3 Md. Inf.	Aug. 1863	1865	2			
	15277.	McKENZIE, Jessie / Ellicott City, Md.	18	18	Private		Patapsco Guards Md.	3 Oct. 1861	17 Oct. 1864	3			
	15278.	Margaret A., widow of / MOCK, Godfrey / Ellicott City, Md.	22	22	Private	E	Md. Inf.	12 Sep. 1861	Oct. 1864	3			
6-3)	15279.	MURPHY, Josiah F. / Ellicott City, Md.	28	29	Corporal	C	3 W. Md.	13 Oct. 1861	13 June 1865	3	8		
6-5)	15280.	Barbara, widow of / MILLER, Joseph / Ellicott City, Md.	37	38	Private		Patapsco Home Guards	not Reenlisted 186	know 186	5			Whole term
	15281.	BAILEY, John D. / Ilchester, Md.	43	44	Private	B	10 Md. Inf.	20 June 1862	Jany 1863		6		
	15282.	HEALY, James H. / Ilchester, Md.	47 / Shot through right hd	48	Private	E	8 Md. Inf.	18 Dec. 1862	11 May 1865	2	5		

Special Schedule. Surviving Soldiers, Sailors, and Marines, and Widows, etc.

Page 1   S. D.: 1 ; E. D.: 413 ; Minor Civil Division.: First Dist. Balto., Co., Md.

	1	2	3	4	5	6	7	8	9 Yrs Mos Dys
	15283. MILLER, August / Ilchester, Md.	48	49	Private		Patapsco Home Guard	16 Oct. 1862	Aug. 1865	2 9
	15284. MYERS, Andrew / Ilchester, Md.	53	54	Private	A	Battery Junior Arter. 6 Mo.	23 June 1863	19 Jany 1864	6

		1		2	3	4	5	6	7	8	9		
	15285.	PORTER, Andrew Ilchester, Md.		58	59	Private Asthma contracted	F	1 Md. Vol.	18 Aug. 1862	3 June 1865	2	8	
	15286.	MacKENZIE, Hiram Ilchester, Md.		59	60	Private	G	Vol. 3 Md. P. H. B.	20 Feby 1864	29 May 1865	1	3	
	15287.	LOGAN, James J. Ilchester, Md.		60	61	Private Shot in leg - & cut on head by saber	B	2 Penn. Calv.	1863	1865	2		
6-6) 8)	15288.	BERRY, Richard A. Ilchester, Md.		62	63	Private	B	Purnell Calv.	Nov. 1861	Nov. 1864	3		
6-10)	15289.	Sarah E., widow of WATERS, Wm. H. Oella, Md.		76	77	Private		Patapsco Home Guards	1861	1864 Reenlisted	3		
	15290.	HOFFMAN, Henry C. Oella, Balto., Co., Md.		87	88	Private	G	4 Md. Vol. Inf.	11 Aug. 1862	31 May 1865	2	9	11
	15291.	KITE, Henry C. Oella, Balto., Co., Md.		87	88	Private		1 Md. Transferred to Purnell Legion	186	186			
6-11)	15292.	Louisa J., widow of PEARCE, Ephrin Oella, Balto., Co., Md.		93	94	Private	I	Inf. 8 Md. Vol.	28 Oct. 1862	8 Aug. 1863		9	
	15293.	PASTER, August Ilchester, Howard Co., Md.	101		102	Private	C	2 Md. Inf.	1 Apr. 1865	25 July 1865		4	
	15294.	Eliza A., widow of McKETTRICK, Samuel Ilchester, Howard Co., Md.	105		106	Private		Patapsco Home Guards	Dec. 1861	186 Died a prisoner at Lynchburg, Va.			
	15295.	SMITHSON, Hezekiah Ilchester, Howard Co., Md.	111		112	Engineer Carpenter	A	2 Dist. Inst.	Aug. 1862	Sept. 1864	2		
	15296.	NEAL, John Ellicott City, Howad Co., Md.	115		116	Private Shot in left hip	K	30 Md. Inft.	Feby 1863	May 1865	2	3	

Special Schedule. Surviving Soldiers, Sailors, and Marines, and Widows, etc.

S. D.: 1 ; E. D.: 413 ; Minor Civil Division.: First Dist. Balto., Co., Md.   Page 2

		1	2	3	4	5	6	7	8	9		
										Yrs	Mos	Dys
6-12)	15297.	Catherine J. Day, formerly wid. of STIER, George A. Oella, Balto., Co., Md.	118	119	Private		Patapsco Home Guards	not 186	know 186			
	15298.	GAYLORD, John Ellicott City, Howd Co., Md.	141	142	Private	F	3 Md. Inf.	16 Sept. 1861	17 Aug. 1865	3	11	

6-13) 15299.	GREENE, Daniel Ellicott City, Howd Co., Md.	150	157	Private	G	39 Md. Inf.	Apr. 1862	Dec. 1865	3		
6-14) 15300.	LEATHERWOOD, Thomas Ellicott City, Howd Co., Md.	153	154	Private Chronic diahrea bleed piles & rhematism - still affect	I	1 Md. Vol.	16 May 1861	30 July 1865	4	1	20
6-16) 15301.	WILSON, William Ellicott City, Howd Co., Md.	172	173	Private	B	10 Md. Inf.	20 June 1863	29 Jan. 1864		7	8
15302.	PERKINS, James Ellicott City, Howard Co., Md.	189	191	Engineer Seaman		Belvedier	186	186			
6-17) 15303.	Laura, widow of HILTON, James Oella, Balto., Co., Md.	182	183	Private	C	13 Md. Inf.	15 Feby 1865	29 May 1865		3	14
15304.	CLARK, George Ellicott City, Md.	216	219	Private Shot in right leg		3 Md. Inf.	186	186			
6-19) 15305.	LOWMAN, France T. Oella, Balto., Co., Md.	236	240	Private Disease of the lung	F	17 U. S. Inf.	186	186			
15306.	HOFF, Joseph Oella, Balto., Co., Md.	242	247	Private Sarcocele	H	21 U. S. Inf.	186	186			
6-20 15307.	MOONEY, Jno. C. Oella, Balto., Co., Md.	246	251	Corporal	F	5 Md. Inf.	14 Oct. 1861	31 Dec. 1863 Veteran			
15308.	SLIVER, William J. Oella, Balto., Co., Md.	278	283	Private	H	8 Md. Inf.	19 Aug. 1862	31 May 1865	2	9	
15309.	McKINZIE, Israel Oella, Balto., Co., Md.	282	287	Sergeant		Patapsco Guard Md.	1 Jany 1862	3 Jany 1865	3		
6-21) 15310.	Annie V. McKenzie, widow of SWEETS, William H. Oella, Balto., Co., Md.	282	287	Private	F	5 Md. Inf.	186	186			

Special Schedule. Surviving Soldiers, Sailors, and Marines, and Widows, etc.

Page

2   S. D.: 1   ; E. D.: 413   ; Minor Civil Division.:   First Dist. Balto., Co., Md.

	1	2	3	4	5	6	7	8	9
									Yrs Mos Dys
15311. LOWE, John W. Oella, Balto., Co., Md.	293	299		Sergent Brights kidney disease	H	8Md. Inf	Oct. 1862	29 Aug. 1863	9
15312. Harriet Buckingham, formerly widow of FARLOW, David Oella, Balto., Co., Md.	305	311		Corporal			186	186 Killed in Antietam Battle	
6-23) 15313. DIFFEY, Victor Oella, Balto., Co., Md.	306	312				Pawpsco Nai Guard	186	186	

6-24)	15314.	GRINE, Henry	315	320	Private	C	1 Md. Inf.	13 Nov. 1864	21 June 1865		7	8
		Ellicott City, Howard Co., Md.			Wounded left side head - gun shot						
	15315.	COOK, James	(25)	26	Private	C	2 D. C. Inf.	Dec. 1862	Nov. 1866	3	11
		Ellicott City, Howard Co., Md.								

Note:-The provision of the act of March 1, 1889, under which this special enumeration of survivors of the war of the rebellion is made, reads as follows:

That said Superintendent shall under the authority of the Secretary of the Interior, cause to be taken on a special schedule of inquiry, according to such form as he may prescribe, the names, organizations, and length of service of those who had served in the Army, Navy, or Marines Corps of the United States in the war of the rebellion, and who are survivors at the time of said inquiry, and the widows of soldiers, sailors, or marines.

The entries concerning each survivor or widow should be carefully and accurately made, so that the printed reports may contain only thoroughly trustworthy information.

Spaces are provided on this special schedule for the entry of fifty names, or more properly, term of service. The spaces are numbered consecutively from 1 to 50, and cover the four pages comprised in each schedule. The inquiries made concerning each survivor or widow call for the repetition of the number of the house and family as returned on the general population schedule (No. 1), the name, rank company, regiment or vessel, date of enlistment, date of discharge, and length of service (in years, months, and days) on the upper half of each page, and the post-office address, disability incurred, and general remarks on the lower half of each page. The column headed "Remarks" is intended to be used to cover any points not included in the forgoing inquires, and which are necessary to a complete statement of a person's term of service in any one organization.

In the case of persons having served in more than one organization, use as many spaces as may be necessary to cover their various terms of service. In the case of widows of deceased soldiers, sailors, or marines, make the entry of her name on the dotted lines, as follows: Mary J., widow of filling out the record of his service during the war, and giving under "post-office address" the Present address of his widow.   BROWN, James H.

Page No. 1
Supervisor's District No. 1
Enumeration District No. 414

Eleventh Census of the United States

SPECIAL SCHEDULE
SURVIVING SOLDIERS, SAILORS, AND MARINES, AND WIDOWS, ETC.

Persons who served in the Army, Navy, and Marine Corps of the United States during the war of the rebellion (who are survivors), and widows of such persons, in   Wethendville   County of   Baltimore
State of   Maryland.   enumerated in June 1890

Samuel J. Bell
Enumerator

	1	2	3	4	5	6	7	8	9 Yrs	Mos	Dys
15316.	BISHOP, John L. Wetheredville Piles	42	44	Captain	E	4 Md. Inf.	14 Aug. 1862	10 Nov. 1863	1	2	27
15317.	BROWN, George W. Wetheredville	58	61	Lieut.	G	Purnell Leg.	4 July 1861	Jan. 1864 Defected in hearing	2	6	
15318.	GINNAMON, Samuel T.	73	78	Private	G	4 Md. Inf.	16 Sept. 1862	31 May 1865	2	8	15
15319.	LEE, John H. Wetheredville Wounded in head injured in spine	77	82	Private	E	43 U. S. C. T.	18 June 1864	20 Nov. 1865	1	5	2
15320.	PARRISH, John H.	82	87	Private	G	4 Md. Inf.	7 Aug. 1862	19 May 1865	2	9	12
15321.	LILLEY, George W. Wetheredville Shot through left side	105	110	Private	G	4 Md. Inf.	4 Aug. 1862	10 June 1865 And now deaf	2	10	6

	1	2	3	4	5	6	7	8	9		
									Yrs	Mos	Dys
15322.	OWENS, Jerome B. Wetheredville	107	112	Private	E	2 Md. Cav.	29 June 1863	4 Jan. 1864	0	11	6
15323.	WARE, William H. Wetheredville	95 Shot in right breast	100	Private	G	4 Md. Inf.	9 Aug. 1862	10 June 1865	2	10	1
15324.	DEAN, William E. Wetheredville	110	115	Private	B	Loudon Ranger	7 May 1864	1 June 1865	1	1	0
15325.	KIDWELL, Charles W. Wetheredville	141	146	Private	H	8 Md. Inf.	24 Nov. 1862	17 Mar. 1863	0	3	21
15326.	JONES, George W. Wetheredville	138	143	Private	G	4 Md. Inf.	9 Aug. 1862	31 May 1865	2	9	22
15327.	MAGNESS, Mosses N. Wetheredville	168	174	Private	B	11 Md. Inf.	10 Feb. 1865	15 June 1865	0	4	5

Special Schedule. Surviving Soldiers, Sailors, and Marines, and Widows, etc.

Page 2   S. D.: 64   ; E. D.: 414   ; Minor Civil Division.: Wetheredville

	1	2	3	4	5	6	7	8	9		
									Yrs	Mos	Dys
15328.	WILMOT, George H. Wetheredville	150	155	Private	C	3 Md. Inf.	Apr. 1864	Sept. 1864	0	6	
15329.	SENTS, Jeremiah Wetheredville	121	126	Private	F	87 Penn. Inf.	2 Sept. 1861	13 Oct. 1864	3	1	11
15330.	PARRISH, George T. Wetheredville	108	113	Private	E	2 Md. Cav.	3 July 1863	21 June 1864	0	11	18
15331.	HALL, Albert G. Wetheredville	106	111	Corporal	D	196 Penn. Inf.	8 July 1863	18 Nov. 1864	1	4	10
15332.	EDMONSTON, Thomas B. Wetheredville	124	129	Private	C	4 Md. Inf.	17 July 1862	31 May 1865	2	9	14
15333.	NORWOOD, Ebenezer Wetheredville	145	150	Private	D	9 Md. Inf.	10 June 1863	Mar. 1864	0	9	

Eleventh Census of the United States

Page No.
Supervisor's District No. 1
Enumeration District No. 415

SPECIAL SCHEDULE
SURVIVING SOLDIERS, SAILORS, AND MARINES, AND WIDOWS, ETC.

Persons who served in the Army, Navy, and Marine Corps of the United States during the war of the rebellion (who are survivors), and widows of such persons, in   2nd Dist.   County of   Baltimore   ,
State of   Maryland.   enumerated in June 1890

C. Ellsworth Upton
Enumerator

	1	2	3	4	5	6	7	8	9		
									Yrs	Mos	Dys
15334.	DANIELS, Jno. H. Lochearn, Balto., Co., Md. Varicocele	8	9	Private	F	4th Md. Inf.	Aug. 1862	June 10 1865 Is nearly disabled	2	10	
15335.	YOUNGER, Lemuel Powhatan, Balto., Co., Md.	17	19	Corporal	E	20th Md. Cav.	9 July 1863	31 Jan. 1864		6	22
15336.	AULT, Conrad Powhatan, Balto., Co., Md.	21	23	Private	D	1st Md. Cav.	12 Nov. 1861	1864 Reinlisted veteran served until 65	2	9	0
15337.	SMITH, Edward Powhatan, Balto., Co., Md.	23	25	Private	F	3 Md. Cav.	16 Apr. 1861	16 Apr. 1864	3	0	0
15338.	RITELEY, Joseph Powhatan, Balto., Co., Md. Paralasis & dropsy	26	28	Private	A	1 Mass. H. A.	28 Mar. 1864 Disabled	16 Aug. 1865	1	4	18
15339.	WAGNER, Henry Powhatan, Balto., Co., Md.	30	32	Private	D	10 Md. Inf.	Apr. 1862	Sept. 1862		6	
15340.	STINAGAN, John Powhatan, Balto., Co., Md.	30	32	Private			186	186			
15341.	RIMMEY, Samuel M. Powhatan, Balto., Co., Md.	32	35	Private	A	11 Md. Inf.	30 Sept. 1864 Re-enlisted veteran	15 June 1865		1	15
15342.	ROBUST, John R. Powhatan, Balto., Co., Md.	34	37	Private	F	10 Md. Inf.	23 June 1863	29 Jan. 1864		1	6
15343.	RIMMEY, William H. Powhatan, Balto., Co., Md.	48	51	Corporal	C	3 Md. Inf.	21 May 1861	Oct. 1864	3	5	
15344.	STIMAX, Isaac C. Powhatan, Balto., Co., Md. Wounded in hand	49	52	Private	F	2 Md. Inf.	3 Dec. 1863	26 Aug. 1864	1	2	23
15345.	TEMPLE, George W. Powhatan, Balto., Co., Md.	52	55	Private	E	2 Md. Cav.	29 June 1863	31 Jany 1864	1	7	21

Special Schedule. Surviving Soldiers, Sailors, and Marines, and Widows, etc.

Page

S. D.: ; E. D.: ; Minor Civil Division.:

	1	2	3	4	5	6	7	8	9		
									Yrs	Mos	Dys
15346.	ZIMMERMAN, William E. Powhatan, Balto., Co., Md.	(Conf)	62	65	Private	Breatheds Bal.	Artillery Stewart Horse	1 June 1863	2 June 1865	2	0	0
15347.	YOUNGER, Richard Powhatan, Balto., Co., Md.	(U. S.)	68	71	Private	I	8 Md. Vol.	29 Oct. 1862	8 Aug. 1863		9	9
15348.	MORRISON, Thomas Powhatan, Balto., Co., Md. Wounded 3 times	(U. S.)	71	73	Private	E	5 Md. Inf.	7 Jany 1862	6 Jany 1865 Disabled by wounds & rheumatism	3	0	0

No.	Name and Residence		House No.	Family No.	Rank	Co.	Regiment	Enlisted	Discharged	Yrs	Mos	Dys
15349.	JONES, Nathan W. Powhatan, Balto., Co., Md.	(U.S.)	75	Bat. 78	Private	Wilcox	Ind.	1861	1863	2		
15350.	DAVIDSON, Edward Powhatan, Balto., Co., Md.	(U.S.)	76	79	Private	E	5 Md. Inf.	1 Nov. 1861	1 Sept. 1865	4		
	Head ear & eye affected 1 yrs Battery F, 5th Reg. Art. Pro. to Cor., acting Sergeant											
15351.	CHILDS, Summerfield Powhatan, Balto., Co., Md.	(U.S.)	79	82	Private	E	2 Md. Cav.	9 July 1863	31 Jan. 1864		6	22
15352.	KIRK, Adam Powhatan, Balto., Co., Md.	(U.S.)	85	88	Private	A	40 N. J. Inf.	6 Oct. 1864	25 July 1865		9	19
15353.	SCHUARD, George Powhatan, Balto., Co., Md.	(U.S.)	75	78	Private	B	Coles Cav.	186 Discharge lost	186	2	3	
15354.	GREMINGER, Henry N. Hebbville, Balto., Co., Md.	(U.S.)	117	120	Corporal	E	57 Penn. Inf.	15 Oct. 1861	29 June 1865	3	9	14
	Corbutus & hemmorrhoids							In prison at Andersonville 6 mos.				
15355.	WAGNER, David Hebbville, Balto., Co., Md.	(U.S.)	127	131	Private	A	5 Md. Inf.	Au. 1861 Reinlisted veteran	Aug. 1865	4	0	0
	Dropsy & knee dislocated by shell at Antietam											
15356.	HARDER, Daniel Rockdale, Balto., Co., Md.	(U.S.)	144	148	Private	B	11 Md. Inf.	1864	1865		6	
15357.	MARRIOTT, William H. Powhatan, Balto., Co., Md.	(U.S.)	158	165	Private	H	8 Md. Inf.	Oct. 1862	July 1863		9	
15358.	ZEIGLER, George Hebbville, Balto., Co., Md.	(U.S.)	185	192	Private	C	68 N. Y. Inf.	12 Aug. 1861 Reinlisted veteran	Dec. 1865	4	3	
	Wounded at Chancellorville & 2 bal. rheumatism incurred Bull Run											
15359.	LIEBUS, Frederick William Hebbville, Balto., Co., Md.	(U.S.)	188	195	Corporal	D	1 Md. Cav.	1 Oct. 1861	18 Oct. 1864	3		17
	Sun stroke, rupture in side											

Special Schedule. Surviving Soldiers, Sailors, and Marines, and Widows, etc.

Page

S. D.:   ; E. D.:   ; Minor Civil Division.:

1	2	3	4	5	6	7	8	9		
								Yrs	Mos	Dys
15360. UPTON, John W. Hebbville, Balto., Co., Md.	208	217	Private	A	3 Md. Inf.	7 Apr. 1865	31 July 1865		3	24
15361. McCABE, John Wetheredville, Balto., Co., Md.	218	228	Private Heart disease contracted in prison at Libby from March	G	1st Md. Inf.	17 May 1861	23 Mar. 1863 Reinlisted in 1st Md. Vet. Cav. in '64	1	10	20
15362. HUMPHREY, John Alberton, Howard Co., Md.	231	241	Private Chills & fevers	G	11 Md. Inf.	1 Feb 1865	20 July 1865		5	20
15363. LUTZ, Charles G. Alberton, Howard Co., Md.	249	260	Private	A	128 N. Y. Inf.	June 1861	1865			

15364.	UPTON, Joshua M.	253	264	Private	B	5 Md. Inf.	28 Nov. 1861	1 Dec. 1864	3		21
	Alberton, Howard Co., Md.		Neuralgia and general debility								
15365.	LIBBY, George W. (Conf)	256	269	Private	A	33 Va. Inf.	June 1861	Apr. 1865	3	10	
	Alberton, Howard Co., Md.										
15366.	HARN, Edwin W. (U. S.)	260	271	Private		2 Md. Inf.	1862	1865	3		
	Alberton, Howard Co., Md.		Feet badly frost bitten								
15367.	WALKER, John T. (U. S.)	263	274	Private	D	1 Md. Inf.	11 Sept. 1861	18 June 1865	3	9	
	Alberton, Howard Co., Md.		Wounded in side & back				Reinlisted in veteran 13 Md. Com. D.				
15368.	HOWARD, William W. (Conf)	267	279	Private	H	5 Va. Inf.	17 Apr. 1861	9 June 1865	4	2	6
	Alberton, Howard Co., Md.		Wounded twice								
15369.	NORTON, Amisey A.	268	280	Private	C	2 Md. Cav.	21 June 1863	6 Feb. 1864			
	Alberton, Howard Co., Md.										
15370.	HAYWORTH, George	270	284	Private	B	3 Md. Inf.	9 Mar. 1863	29 May 1863		2	20
	Alberton, Howard Co., Md.										
15371.	BORTLE, John E.	273	281	Private	I	103 Ohio Inf.	7 Aug. 1862	13 June 1865	2	10	
	Alberton, Howard Co., Md.		Ruptured in stomach								
15372.	JOHNSON, William (col.)	282	299	Private	C	24 Pa. Inf. (col)	1862	1865	3		
	Alberton, Howard Co., Md.		Eresipelis in eyes								
	Carl Earnst alias										
15373.	PFEIFFER, George E.	274	288	Private	C	45 N. Y. Inf.	June 1862	Sept. 1865	3	2	
	Alberton, Howard Co., Md.		Rheumatism				In 3 Battles				

Special Schedule. Surviving Soldiers, Sailors, and Marines, and Widows, etc.

Page

S. D.: ; E. D.: ; Minor Civil Division.:

		1	2	3	4	5	6	7	8	9
										Yrs Mos Dys
15374.	STIMIX, Isaac C. (Conf)				Private	I	2 Md. Inf.	June 1863	186	
	Powhatan									
15375.	*QUEEN, Andrew	80	83	Sol				186	186	
	2nd Dist., Baltimore, Md.									

Note:-The provision of the act of March 1, 1889, under which this special enumeration of survivors of the war of the rebellion is made, reads as follows:

That said Superintendent shall under the authority of the Secretary of the Interior, cause to be taken on a special schedule of inquiry, according to such form as he may prescribe, the names, organizations, and length of service of those who had served in the Army, Navy, or Marines Corps of the United States in the war of the rebellion, and who are survivors at the time of said inquiry, and the widows of soldiers, sailors, or marines.

The entries concerning each survivor or widow should be carefully and accurately made, so that the printed reports may contain only thoroughly trustworthy information.

Spaces are provided on this special schedule for the entry of fifty names, or more properly, term of service. The spaces are numbered consecutively from 1 to 50, and cover the four pages comprised in each schedule. The inquiries made concerning each survivor or widow call for the repetition of the number of the house and family as returned on the general population schedule (No. 1), the name, rank company, regiment or vessel, date of enlistment, date of discharge, and length of service (in years, months, and days) on the upper half of each page, and the post-office address, disability incurred, and general remarks on the lower half of each page. The column headed "Remarks" is intended to be used to cover any points not included in the forgoing inquires, and which are necessary to a complete statement of a person's term of service in any one organization.

In the case of persons having served in more than one organization, use as many spaces as may be necessary to cover their various terms of service. In

the case of widows of deceased soldiers, sailors, or marines, make the entry of her name on the dotted lines, as follows: Mary J., widow of
filling out the record of his service during the war, and giving under "post-office address" the Present address of his widow.   BROWN, James H.

Page No.
Supervisor's District No. 1st
Enumeration District No. 415-A

Eleventh Census of the United States

SPECIAL SCHEDULE
SURVIVING SOLDIERS, SAILORS, AND MARINES, AND WIDOWS, ETC

Persons who served in the Army, Navy, and Marine Corps of the United States during the war of the rebellion (who are survivors), and widows of such persons, in   Granile - 2nd Dist.   County of   Baltimore
State of   Maryland.   enumerated in June 1890

Francis Sanderson
Enumerator

	1	2	3	4	5	6	7	8	9
									Yrs Mos Dys
15376.	DAVIS, Robert	26	28	Private	I	39 U. S. Col. Infantry	Nov. 16 1862	Nov. 16 1864	1 4
	Granite - Balto., Co., Md.		Chronic rheumatism in limbs						
15377.	KEENIE, Ezra	19	21	Private	B	7 Md. Inf.	Aug. 18 1862	May 31 1865	1 9 12
	Granite - Balto., Co., Md.		Rheumatism & partial blindness						
15378.	AILER, Peter	51	55	Seaman		Under Admiral Amen	186	186	
	Granite - Balto., Co., Md.							Owner in Baltimore & papers not home	
15379.	MASON, Robert K.	29	31	Private	C	1st Maryland Infantry	May 31 1862	May 31 1863	1
	Granite - Balto., Co., Md.								

Page No.
Supervisor's District No. 1
Enumeration District No. 416

Eleventh Census of the United States

SPECIAL SCHEDULE
SURVIVING SOLDIERS, SAILORS, AND MARINES, AND WIDOWS, ETC

Persons who served in the Army, Navy, and Marine Corps of the United States during the war of the rebellion (who are survivors), and widows of such persons, in   County of   Baltimore
State of   Maryland.   enumerated in June 1890

Harry G. Luttgerduy
Enumerator

	1	2	3	4	5	6	7	8	9
									Yrs Mos Dys
15380.	BARTHOLOME, Christian	13	13	Private	C	5th Md.	Sep. 12 1861	Dec. 31 1863	4
	Harrisonville, Md.		Eyesight afficted					Reinlisted as a Veteran Vol.	
15381.	Roxanna V., widow of REYNOLDS, Alfred D.	17	17	Lieut.	F	1st Md.	5 Apr. 1861	Apr. 1 1864	3
	Riesterstown, Md.							Husband killed Battle Weldon R. R.	
15382.	WEST, Henry	28	28	Private	A	6th Md. Vol.	Aug. 11 1862	Jany 24 1865	3
	Harrisonville, Md.		Rupture & piles				Have heart trouble		

Page -14-

15383.	COLLINS, George (col) North Branch, Md.	36	36	Private	B	30 Md.	Sep.	1864	Dec. 24 1865	1	4	
		General disability										
15384.	SHIRLEY, William H. Harrisonville, Md.	92	92	Private	F	5th Md.	Nov. 8 1862		Sept. 15 1865	3		
		Spinal affection							Enlisted twice			
15385.	FRANK, George B. Randallstown, Md.	103	103	Private	I	10th Md. Inf.	Jun. 30 1863		Jan. 29 1864		6	29
		Frost bitten feet										
15386.	HEEWARA, John Harrisonville, Md.		120	120	Private	D	2nd Md. Vet.	Dec. 1 1864	July 17 1865		7	17
									Discharged at close of war			
	James H. Watts, alias				V.	don't know						
15387.	COLE, James (col) Granite, Md.	137	137	Private	D	2nd U. S. Vo.	Aug.	186	Jany 16 1866	don't know		
									Lost his discharge			
15388.	BROWN, Enoch Granite, Md.	161	168	Private	F	1st Md. Vol.	Feby 20 1864		July 2 1865	1	4	12
		None							Twice enlisted			
15389.	HAMILTON, Joseph A. Granite, Md.	161	168	Private		Balto. Battery Light Artillery	Aug. 11 1862		May 18 1865			
		Shortness of breath							Discharged for disability			
15390.	PHILLIPS, George Granite, Md.	154	159	Private	E	5 Md. Vol.		1861	July 1 1865			
		Piles							No date on discharge			
15391.	JOHNSON, Joseph T. Granite, Md.	209	219	Private	B	11 Md. Vol.	May	1863	1865	about 2 yrs		
		Cut in the knee by an ax							Cant give exact dates above			

Special Schedule. Surviving Soldiers, Sailors, and Marines, and Widows, etc.

Page

S. D.: 1 ; E. D.: 416 ; Minor Civil Division.: Second district

1	2	3	4	5	6	7	8	9			
									Yrs	Mos	Dys
15392. YINGLING, William H. Hernwood, Md.	226	236	Private	G	1st Reg. Md. Vet Vol.	Dec. 4 1862	July 2 1865		2	6	28
Dyspepsia incident to exposure											
15393. BARNES, Uriah North Branch, Md.	230	240	Private	C	9 Reg. Md. Inf.	July 2 1863	Feb. 23 1864 In hospital 60 days		0	7	21
Typoid fever incident to exposure											

Page No. 1
Supervisor's District No. 1
Enumeration District No. 416-A

Eleventh Census of the United States

SPECIAL SCHEDULE
SURVIVING SOLDIERS, SAILORS, AND MARINES, AND WIDOWS, ETC

Persons who served in the Army, Navy, and Marine Corps of the United States during the war of the rebellion (who are survivors), and widows of such persons, in   2nd district   County of   Baltimore   ,
State of   Maryland.   enumerated in June 1890

Wm. H. Harker
Enumerator

	1	2	3	4	5	6	7	8	9		
									Yrs	Mos	Dys
15394.	SAUMENIG, Henry Hernwood	6	6	Hospital Steward			13 June 1862	13 June 1865 1st enlisted in 1852 in service when war began finally discharged 1870	3		
15395.	STANFIELD, Thomas B. Harrissonville	12	13	Private	F	4 M. Vol.	11 Aug. 1862	10 June 1865	2	10	

Page No. 1
Supervisor's District No. 1st
Enumeration District No. 417

Eleventh Census of the United States

SPECIAL SCHEDULE
SURVIVING SOLDIERS, SAILORS, AND MARINES, AND WIDOWS, ETC.

Persons who served in the Army, Navy, and Marine Corps of the United States during the war of the rebellion (who are survivors), and widows of such persons, in 2nd Dist. County of Baltimore, State of Maryland. enumerated in June 1890

Henry S. Jean
Enumerator

	1	2	3	4	5	6	7	8	9		
									Yrs	Mos	Dys
15396.	VIRMILLION, Lorenzo Rockdale, Baltimore Co., Md.	31	31	Private	E	3 Md. Inf.	186 Don't remember date of enlistment	June 10 1865	1	8	0
15397.	CROSS, Nicklos Randalstown, Maryland Co., of Baltimore	38	38	Private	H	10 Md. Inf.	186 Don't remember dates	186			
15398.	PICKETT, William Owings Mills, Baltimore Co., Md.	46	46	Private Kidney dease	H	16 Md. H. Art.	1 Jan. 1864	21 Aug. 1865	1	8	
15399.	FREASMAN, Joseph H. McDonah, Balto., Co., Md.	2		Private		Inf.	186 Don't remember dates don't know anything	186			
15400.	NORIS, Charles W. Randalstown, Balto., Co., Md.	55	55	Private	H	4 Md. Inf.	186 Don't no dates	186			
15401.	DAVIS, Henry Randalstown, Md.	59	59	Private	H	5 Md. Inf.	186 Don't no dates	186			
15402.	TOLBERT, Samuel L. Rockdale, Balto., Co., Md.	73	74	(Lutenet) Lieut	C	4 Md. Inf.	1 Aug. 1862	Sep. 12 1863	1	3	10
15403.	WHITEN, William H. Rockdale, Balto., Co., Md.	87	88	Private	H	28 Indiana Inf.	1 Aug. 1864	Jan 8 1868	2	4	0
15404.	SULLIVAN, George W. Pikesville, Balto., Co., Md.	120	121	Private	B	3 Md. Inf.	8 Mch 1865	May 8 1865	3		

Over - page

Special Schedule. Surviving Soldiers, Sailors, and Marines, and Widows, etc.

Page

S. D.: 1st ; E. D.: 417 ; Minor Civil Division.: Md.

1	2	3	4	5	6	7	8	9 (Yrs Mos Dys)
15405. BANBERGER, William W. Lochern Balto., Co., Md.	90	91	Col.		5 Md. Vet. Vol. Inf. Gun shot wound both lungs	9 Oct. 1861	25 Sep. 186 Ball still remang in lung	3 10 6

Page No. 1
Supervisor's District No. 1
Enumeration District No. 418

Eleventh Census of the United States

SPECIAL SCHEDULE
SURVIVING SOLDIERS, SAILORS, AND MARINES, AND WIDOWS, ETC.

Persons who served in the Army, Navy, and Marine Corps of the United States during the war of the rebellion (who are survivors), and widows of such persons, in   1st Precinct 3rd District   County of   Baltimore   ,
State of   Maryland.   enumerated in June 1890

Samuel Yardley
Enumerator

1	2	3	4	5	6	7	8	9 (Yrs Mos Dys)
15406. Rebecca F., widow of LOVEJOY, Perley R. Mt. Washington, Baltimore Co., Md.	26	26	Captain	G	9 Md. Inf. Shot through left arm & shoulder	10 Jany 1863	4 Feb. 1864 Deceased Oct. 23 1889 from effect of wound received in service	6 25
15407. Annie A. Brooks, wid. of REMPEL, F. F. Mt. Washington, Baltimore Co., Md.	29	29	Colonel		58 Ohio Inf.	unknown 186	unknown 186 Date of enlistment & discharge & length of service unknown	
15408. Mary B., widow of POND, Erastus Mt. Washington, Baltimore Co., Md.	29	29	Captain		unknown No information obtain then above	unknown 186	unknown 186 He was probably wagon master	
15409. QUINN, Edward H. Mt. Washington, Baltimore Co., Md.	30	30	Major Regt. Surgeon None		15 Ky Inf.	2 Aug. 1862	14 Jan. 1865 Now maimed from amputation of left leg since leaving service	2 5 12
15410. RITTER, Oliver R. Mt. Washington, Baltimore Co., Md.	37	37	Private None	I	8 Md. Inf.	unknown 186	unknown 186 Now with chronic rheumatism	
15411. BRENIZE, Joseph K. Mt. Washington, Baltimore Co., Md.	41	41	Private None	A	50 Pa. Inf.	10 Mch 1865	3 July 1865 In good health now	3 23
15412. GARTSIDE, John W. Mt. Washington, Baltimore Co., Md.	49	49	Private None	I	1 Md. Inf.	unknown 186	unknown 186 Now with defective sight	

15413.	TRUSTY, Thomas W. 63 Mt. Washington, Baltimore Co., Md.	63 Shot through right breast & first finger on left hand	Private	I	4 Md. Inf.	unk Sept. 1863	unk Sept. 1865 Now with defective sight right eye	
15414.	Sarah F., widow of FORDWELL, William A. 73 Mt. Washington, Baltimore Co., Md.	73 Prisoner Bell Island shot in right leg	Private	I	4 Md. Inf.	unknown 186 Died at Bells Island	unknown 186	unknown
15415.	PENNIMAN, Edward J. 91 Mt. Washington, Baltimore Co., Md.	91 No disability	Private	C	10 Md. Inf.	unk June 1863	unk April 1864	
15416.	STEVENSON, William H. H. 96 Mt. Washington, Baltimore Co., Md.	96 No disability except catarrh	Private	B	13 Md. Inf.	26 Feb. 1865	29 May 1865 Now with chronic catarrah	3 3
15417.	WOODCOCK, Theodore W. 125 Mt. Washington, Baltimore Co., Md.	126 Wounded in testicles	Sargeant	A	Coles Md. Cav.	unknown 186 Enlistment & discharge not known	unknown 186	

Special Schedule. Surviving Soldiers, Sailors, and Marines, and Widows, etc.

Page 2 S. D.: 1st ; E. D.: 418 ; Minor Civil Division.: 1st Presenct 3rd Dist., Md.

	1	2	3	4	5	6	7	8	9
									Yrs Mos Dys
15418.	DONOVAN, Patrick 119 Mt. Washington, Balto., Co., Md.	120	Flesh wound left leg	Marine		Labini	9 Feb. 1865	186 Now perfectly well	
15419.	YATES, Jr. Matthew 145 Mt. Washington, Balto., Co., Md.	146 None		Private	A	30 Md. Inf.	186	186 Time of service unknown	
15420.	GRAHAM, John T. 58 Mt. Washington, Balto., Co., Md.	58 None		1st Lieut.		&B Q. M. Purnell Legion	17 Sept. 1861	13 July 1862	9 26
15421.	YATES, Lemuel A. 156 Brooklandville, Baltimore Co., Md.	157 None		Private	D. C. C	6th Batn. Md.	11 April 1861	11 July 1861 Now with chronic rhumatism	3
15422.	STRICKLAND, William 163 Mt. Washington, Baltimore Co., Md.	164 Chronic diarrhoea		Private	A	4 U. S. Ar.	16 Feb. 1864	16 Feb. 1867 The disease contracted during war	3
15423.	SMITH, Peter 164 Mt. Washington, Baltimore Co., Md.	165 Mashed testicles in a charge	3rd	Corporal	E	13 U. S. H. Ar.	unknown 1865	unknown 1865 Enlisted in Louisville, Ky.	unknown
15424.	GITTINGS, Isaac 185 Melvale, Baltimore Co., Md.	186 None		Private	F	39 Md. Inf.	Mch 1864	Dec. 1865	
15425.	Ansinette, widow of BISHOP, Thomas 177 Melvale, Baltimore Co., Md.	178 Shot in thumb		Corporal		Md. Inf.	186	186 Dis. papers in hands of pension agent.	
15426.	*REED, Annie J. widow 42 Mt. Washington, Baltimore Co.	32					186	186	

Page No.
Supervisor's District No. 1
Enumeration District No. 419

Eleventh Census of the United States

SPECIAL SCHEDULE
SURVIVING SOLDIERS, SAILORS, AND MARINES, AND WIDOWS, ETC.

Persons who served in the Army, Navy, and Marine Corps of the United States during the war of the rebellion (who are survivors), and widows of such persons, in 2nd Precinct of 3rd District County of Baltimore, State of Maryland. enumerated in June 1890

Francis Sanderson
Enumerator

	1	2	3	4	5	6	7	8	9		
									Yrs	Mos	Dys
15427.	REIF, Charles F. Arlington, Balto., Co., Md.	241	253	Corporal Ruptured	B	10 Maryland Infantry	20 June 1863	20 Jan. 1864	0	7	9
15428.	PRESTON, Wesley black Mount Washington, Balto., Co., Md.	230	242	Private Struck by shell in head	F	7 Reg. U. S. Calvary	Sep. 27 1863	May 31 1865 Receives pension	1	5	3
15429.	BELL, Joshua Wetheredsville, Balto., Co., Md.	38	40	Private Fistula & rheumatism		papers lost & can not tell	186 Thinks he was in Home Guards - cant find out whether he was in Army	186	0	0	0
15430.	BALL, T. Savell Pikesville, Balto., Co., Md.	6	8	Private None	B	10 Maryland Infantry	June 17 1863	Jan. 29 1864		7	12
15431.	McCULLEY, John H. Howardville, Balto., Co., Md.	5	7	Private Flesh wounds on body (healed)	Artillery A	1st Maryland L.	Sept. 15 1861	Nov. 8 1864	3	1	24
15432.	NICHOLS, Henry H. Howardville, Balto., Co., Md.	13	15	Private Sound	E	28 Indiana Infantry	Oct. 16 1863	Sept. 16 1865	1	11	0
15433.	JONES, James H. Wetherdsville, Balto., Co., Md.	57	60	Private Sound	K	7 Maryland Infantry	June 20 1863	July 7 1865	2	0	17
15434.	WEED, David M. Arlington, Balto., Co., Md.	67	70	Sergeant Asthma	A	2 U. S. Calvary	Nov. 26 1862	Nov. 26 1865	3	0	0
15435.	ANDSON, Steven J. Arlington, Balto., Co., Md.	122	126	Private Rheumatism	I	Infantry 150 New York	Sept. 12 1862	Dec. 12 1862	0	3	0
15436.	ENSOR, Daniel E. Arlington, Balto., Co., Md.	108	112	Sergeant Sound	H	1st Maryland Infantry	May 16 1861	July 3 1865	4	1	18
15437.	CHILDS, Benjamin F. Arlington, Balto., Co., Md.	145	148	Private Right thumb shot away	C	1st U. S. Infantry	1861 July 28 1855	62 Aug. 5 1857 Receiving pensioned	2	0	7
15438.	WAMSLEY, John S. Arlington, Balto., Co., Md.	148	151	Sergeant 1st Left Sound	A D	4 Maryland Inft. 25 D. S. Inf.	M 1862 1864	1864 1864	2 2		

Page -19-

Special Schedule. Surviving Soldiers, Sailors, and Marines, and Widows, etc.

S. D.: 3 ; E. D.: 419 ; Minor Civil Division.: Maryland

1	2	3	4	5	6	7	8	9 Yrs	Mos	Dys
			Private	C	114 Illinois Artillery	July 20 1863	July 31 1865	2	0	11
15439. MORIARTY, Matthew C. Arlington Balto., Co., Md.	141	144	Private General disability	B	4 U. S. Lig. H.	Aug. 1 1865	Sept. 1 1871 Receives pension	6	0	32
15440. KEENE, Charles E. Flag & Eagle Club Balto., City, Md.	203	207 None	Infantry Private	F	4 Maryland	Aug. 15 1862	May 15 1865	2	10	0
15441. LEWIS, Charles black Pikesville Balto., Co., Md.	3	3	Infantry Private Rheumatism	G	1 Maryland	Apr. 18 1862	Oct. 18 1865	3	6	0
15442. SMITH, George W. black Howardville Balto., Co., Md.	74	78 None	Private	E	8 Penna. Infty	Sept. 16 1862	Dec. 20 1865	3	3	4
Sarah J. Deakins, widow of 15443. HOLLIDAY, Edward black Arlington Balto., Co., Md.	74	78	Infantry Private Rheumatism & very poor, papers lost	B	1 Maryland	May 1862	May 1864 I know him as a man & soldier but don't know what regiment he was in for sure. This is her recollection of time	2	0	0
15444. BROWN, Robert M. black Arlington Balto., Co., M.	86	90	Col. Infantry Sergeant Wounded in side	E	7 U. S. Regiment	Sept. 27 1863	June 7 1865 Papers filed for pension	1	8	11
15445. THOMAS, Gustus black Arlington Balto., Co., Md.	3	3	Private			186	186 Papers lost & man at sea			
15446. ROGERS, William F. Arlington Balto., Co., Md.	207	211	Captain Retired		U. S. Navy	186	186 Being absent could not get information			
15447. *SAHERS, Mary E. widow 2nd Precinct Baltimore, Md.	46	49	U. S. Sol.			186	186			
15448. *HELLEM, Isaac W. H. 2nd Precinct Baltimore, Md.	97	101	Soldier			186	186			

Eleventh Census of the United States

Page No. 1
Supervisor's District No. 1
Enumeration District No. 420

SPECIAL SCHEDULE
SURVIVING SOLDIERS, SAILORS, AND MARINES, AND WIDOWS, ETC.

Persons who served in the Army, Navy, and Marine Corps of the United States during the war of the rebellion (who are survivors), and widows of such persons, in Third Precinct of 3rd District County of Baltimore , State of Maryland. enumerated in June 1890

B. S. Woolston
Enumerator

	1	2	3	4	5	6	7	8	9		
									Yrs	Mos	Dys
15449.	CHANY, John Mt. Washington, Balto., Co., Md.	324	339	Private	B	28 Md. Inf.	Sept. 1863	July 1865	1	10	
15450.	SMITH, John Rockland, Balto., Co., Md.	7	12	Private	B	1 Md. Inf.	Augt. 1862	July 1864	2	10	
15451.	CHENOWETH, William H. Brooklinville, Balto., Co., Md.	11	16	Private	O	Purnell Cav.	Dec. 1861	Dec. 1864	3	0	4
15452.	JANNEY, Thomas (Conf) Stevenson, Balto., Co., Md.	40	45	Corral	H	5th Son	June 1861	July 1863		2	1
15453.	Hancock Com. DORSEY, Martin Stevenson, Balto., Co., Md.	46	51	Private	H	1 U. S. Vol.	1861	1865	4		
15454.	AGNUS, Felix Stevenson, Balto., Co., Md.	55	60	Brig. Genl. U. S. Vols. Right shoulder shot away		5th Infantry 19th Corp 165 N. Y.	19 Apl 1861	Sept. 1865	4	5	
15455.	Ellen M., widow of MASON, John T. Stevenson, Balto., Co., Md.	66	71	Private		28th Indiana	186	186			
15456.	RUFF, Jacob F. Stevenson, Balto., Co., Md.	73	78	Private Injured in leg		1st Md. Cav.	1861	1864 Prisoner	3		
15457.	Nancy Brown, widow of BROWN, Chas. H. Stevenson, Balto., Co., Md.	68	73	Private	A	19th Reg.	died in 186 service	186			
15458.	REMMEL, John H. Stevenson, Balto., Co., Md.	87	92	Private	9	Eastern Shore 2nd Md. Vol.	1861	1865 Re-enlisted veteran	end of war		
15459.	BOYLE, Thomas B. Mt. Washington, Balto., Co., Md.	112	117	Wounded in scalp		Benton	1861	1865			
15460.	GRIFFIN, Matthew Luke Pikesville, Balto., Co. Md.	147	153	Private		Lieut Robt. W. Spinney Regt. of H. S. Colored Troops	5 Oct. 1864	14 Nov. 1865	1	1	9

Special Schedule. Surviving Soldiers, Sailors, and Marines, and Widows, etc.

Page 2 S. D.: 1 ; E. D.: 420 ; Minor Civil Division.: Baltimore 3 Precinct 3rd Dist., Maryland

1	2	3	4	5	6	7	8	9
								Yrs Mos Dys

15461.	BRECKENRIDGE, Robert Pikesville, Balto., Co.	202	215	Private	H	29th U. S. Col. Inf.	Oct. 20 1864	Dec. 8 1865	1	1	18
15462.	Nancy, widow of SMALLWOOD, Edward Pikesville, Balto., Co.	202	215					186		186	
15463.	Mary, widow of PRESLEY, John Pikesville, Balto., Co.	174	181					186		186	
15464.	Elizabeth, widow of HOLMES, Pikesville, Balto., Co.	203	216					186		186	
15465.	BRENBERGER, John E. Pikesville, Balto., Co.	219	232	Artillery Private	H	2nd Penn. Heavy	Feb. 25 1864	Jan. 5 1866	1	10	11
15466.	Jane B., widow of USSEN, George Pikesville, Balto., Co.	319 Wounded in left foot	334	Private	J	4th U. S. C. T.			186		186	
15467.	*STEVENS, Alexander Third precinct, Balto., Co.	150	156	U. S. Navy					186		186	
15468.	widow U. S. Sol. *MILLS, Amanda Third precinct, Balto., Co.	227	240	U. Sol.					186		186	
15469.	*CARRINGTON, Josiah Third precinct, Balto., Co.	58	63	Hostle Sol.					186		186	
15470.	*MARTIN, Lewis Third precinct, Balto., Co.	243	257	Sol. U. S.					186		186	
15471.	widow of U. S. Sol. *HALL, Susan	308	323	Widow Sol. U. S.					186		186	
15472.	*CHANY, John	324	339	Sol. U. S.					186		186	

Page No. 1
Supervisor's District No. 1
Enumeration District No. 421

Eleventh Census of the United States

SPECIAL SCHEDULE
SURVIVING SOLDIERS, SAILORS, AND MARINES, AND WIDOWS, ETC.

Persons who served in the Army, Navy, and Marine Corps of the United States during the war of the rebellion (who are survivors), and widows of such persons, in County of Baltimore ,
State of Maryland. enumerated in June 1890

R. Edwin Hook
Enumerator

1   2   3   4   5   6   7   8   9

No.	Name	2	3	Rank	5	Company/Unit	Enlisted	Discharged	Yrs	Mos	Dys
15473.	SHOOK, Daniel J. Owing Mills	12	12	Private	A	13 Md. Inf.	15 Feby 1865	29 May 1865		3	14
15474.	WALTER, John W. Owing Mills	14	14	Corporal	I	122 Pa. Inf.	186	186		9	
15475.	Catharine Moore, widow MOORE, Henry W. Owing Mills	15	15	Seaman		Saratoga	186	186			
15476.	MORROW, Joseph Owing Mills	31	31	Private	F	10 Md. Inf.	8 July 1863	23 Jany 1864		6	23
15477.	BRUMMEL, Joseph Owing Mills	36	36	Private			June 1862	186 No other information can be had			
15478.	TASE, Martin Owing Mills	40	40	Private	H	10 Md. Inf.	29 June 1863	29 Jany 1864		7	
15479.	MORROW, Hezekiah Owing Mills	41	41	Corporal	F	10 Md. Inf.	29 June 1863	29 Jany 1864		7	
15480.	GROFF, Benjamin F. Owing Mills	33	33				186	186 Can give no information as to rank, etc.			
15481.	DEVOUGES, Victor P. Owing Mills	57	57	Private	A	2 Md. Cal.	22 June 1863	26 Jany 1864		7	4
15482.	John F. Shray, alias ROSELIEP, John Owing Mills	61	61 Shot in head and arm	Private	C	16 Penn. Cav.	22 Oct. 1862	11 Aug. 1865	2	10	
15483.	Annie M. Fairfax, formerly widow of SCOTT, Edward Owing Mills	63	63	Sergt.	F	10 Virg.	1863 All papers lost	186			
15484.	WATKINS, Joseph Owing Mills	70	70			Virg.	186	186 Can give no other information			

Special Schedule. Surviving Soldiers, Sailors, and Marines, and Widows, etc.

Page

S. D.: 1 ; E. D.: 421 ; Minor Civil Division.:

1	2	3	4	5	6	7	8	9		
								Yrs	Mos	Dys
15485. HANNA, James R. Reistertown	77 Rhuematism	77	Private	B	8 Md. Inf.	Aug. 1862	June 1865	2	9	
15486. DORSEY, Robert Reistertown	86	86	Private	D	38 U. S. Inf.	March 1864	April 1865	1		
15487. NAFE, Henry Owing Mills	111	112	Private	D	13 Md. Inf.	18 Jany 1864	29 May 1865	1	3	11

Page No.
Supervisor's District No. 1
Enumeration District No. 422

Eleventh Census of the United States

SPECIAL SCHEDULE
SURVIVING SOLDIERS, SAILORS, AND MARINES, AND WIDOWS, ETC.

Persons who served in the Army, Navy, and Marine Corps of the United States during the war of the rebellion (who are survivors), and widows of such persons, in 14th Districl County of Baltimore, State of Maryland. enumerated in June 1890

Robert J. Henry, M. D.
Enumerator

1	2	3	4	5	6	7	8	9 Yrs Mos Dys
15488. TRAINOR, Joseph Woodensburg, Md.	18 None	18	Pri.	B	Purnell Legion Md.	10 Sept. 1861	Oct. 24 1864	3 1 14
15489. WILLIAMS, John J. Glyndon, Md.	46 Sun stroke piles diarrhoea	48	Sergt.	G	Purnell Legion Md.	13 Sept. 1861	Oct. 24 1864 Malarial poisoning &c.	3 1 11
15490. SMITH, George Glyndon, Md.	33 Rheumatism, bronchitis & lung disease	35	Pri.	H	Purnell Legion Md.	Dec. 1861	Nov. 1863 Aug. 19, 1865 & S. O. No. 29 Hd. Qrs. Dept. Miss.	2
15491. BURNS, Wm. D. Glyndon, Md.	64 Rheumatism	66	Pri.	G	3 Md. Cav.	18 Sept. 1863	Sept. 7 1865	3
15492. KELLEY, William H. Glyndon, Md.	65	67	Corpl	D	7 Md. Inf.	Nov. 1862	186 Supposed deserted	
15493. CHINWORTH, William Glyndon, Md.	84 Rheumatism inj. back	85	Pri.	D	7 Md. Inf.	19 Aug. 1862 Exp. term service	May 31 1865	2 9 12
15494. KEMP, Dr. J. McKendre Glyndon, Md.	90	91	Asst. Surgeon		1 Md. E. S. Inf.	9 Apl 1863	Feb. 4 1865	
15495. √KEMP, Dr. J. McKendre Glenullarrio, Md.	90	91	Asst. Surgeon		11 Md. Inf.	10 Feb. 1865	Aug. 1 1865	
15496. MADDEN, Amos St. Georges, Md.	99 Injured in service by tent pole, epilepsy	101	Pri.	G	28 U. S. Col. Inf.	9 July 1864	Nov. 8 1865	
15497. CONSTANTINE, Richard St. Georges, Md.	101	103	Pri.	C	13 Md. Inf.	27 Feb. 1865	29 May 1865 Sp. Order 120 Hd. Qrs. Mid. Mil. Dept. May 19/65 8th A. C.	
15498. Harriet, widow of CAMPBELL, Andrew Glyndon, Md.	115	117	(unknown)			186	186	
15499. BRUMMEL, David O. Boring, Md.	131	133	(could not ascertain)			186	186	

Special Schedule. Surviving Soldiers, Sailors, and Marines, and Widows, etc.

Page

S. D.: 1 ; E. D.: 422 ; Minor Civil Division.:

	1	2	3	4	5	6	7	8	9
									Yrs Mos Dys
15500.	HARRIS, Richard Towblesburg, Md. Heart disease	138	141	Pri.	I	6 Md. Inf.	14 Aug. 1862 Disability on half	20 June 1865	2 10 7
15501.	NELSON, Samuel Boring, Md. Back injured - ruptured	149	150	Pri.	H	30 U. S. C. Inf.	17 Mar. 1864 S. O. # 249 Hd. Qrs. Dept. HC Nov. 24th 1865	10 Dec. 1865	
15502.	BOLTE, Henry Boring, Md.	152	153	Pri.	H	3 Md. Inf.	27 Mar. 1865 S. O. # 120 Mid. Dept., Balto., May 19th 1865	29 May 1865	
15503.	HUNT, William T. Glyndon, Md. Rheumatism after Antietam	159	161	Pri.	I	11 Md. Inf.	21 Aug. 1862 S. O. # 138 Mid. Dept., Balto., June 8th /65	15 June 1865	
15504.	CHINWORTH, John H. Glyndon, Md. alias Frank B. Dorsey	165	167	Pri. Pri.	D K	7 Md. Inf. 2 N. H. Inf.	30 Aug. 1862 1863	31 May 1865	
15505.	BUCHANNAN, George Boring, Md. None	180	185	Pri.	B	12 N. H. Inf.	May 1864 Reinlisted veteran 12th N. H. Co. 2nd N. H.	Dec. 1865	
15506.	NESS, Samuel R. Boring, Md. Piles	182	187	Pri.	H	200 Pa. Inf.	13 Aug. 1864 Dischd, orders War Dept. May 17 & 18 1865	30 May 1865	
15507.	BATTLE, George Boring, Md. R. inguinal & hernia	183	188	Pri.	H	30 U. S. C. Inf.	17 Mar. 1864 S. O. # 249 Hd. Qrs. Dept. H C. Nov. 24 1865	10 Dec. 1865	
15508.	TAWNEY, Andrew C. Boring, Md. Chronic rheumatism	184	189	Pri.	H	Inf 3 Md. P. H. B.	27 Mar. 1865 S. O. # 120 Hd. Qrs. Mid. Md. Dept. Balto., May 19th /65	29 May 1865	
15509.	WRIGHT, William S. Towblesburg, Md. Wounded Hatchers Run, Va., Feb. 6/65 Loss index & 1st finger & 2 finger	194	199	Pri.	D	11 Pa. Inf.	Feb. 1864	14 June 1865	
15510.	CALDWELL, John J. Dover, Md. Ch. rheumatism (General)	200	205	Asst. Surgeon			Aug. 1862 Contracted in U. S. Service at Elmira Prison Few medical officers 12,000 prisoners N. Y. Barracks.	July 1866	
15511.	BEAVER, Oliver Dover, Md.	204	210	Pri.	F	13 Md. Inf.	Sept. 1864	5 June 1865	
15512.	HENRY, Robert J. (M. D.) Glyndon, Md. Malarial poisoning resulting	209	215	Medical Cadet U. S. A.			9 June 1864 Contracted in service at	9 June 1865	1 0 0

	1								
15513.	√HENRY, Robert J. (M. D.) 209 215 A. Asst Surgeon U. S. A. 26 Mar. 1866 26 Aug. 1866 0 5 0								
	Glyndon, Md. Disease liver, rheumatism, endocarditis U. S. Quarantine Sta. Dog Iland Florida June & July 1866								

Special Schedule. Surviving Soldiers, Sailors, and Marines, and Widows, etc.

Page

S. D.:   1   ; E. D.:   422   ; Minor Civil Division.:

	1	2	3	4	5	6	7	8	9
									Yrs Mos Dys
				Pri.	B	7th U. S. Inf.	24 Oct. 1864	24 Oct. 1867	
				Pri.	113th	2 Bat. Vet. Res. C.	14 Sept. 1863	8 June 1864	
15514.	FOLEY, John	232	241	Pri.	F	7 U. S. Inf.	5 July 1860	4 Mar. 1863	
	Woodensbury, Md.	G. S. W. Right femur							
15515.	UPPERCO, Benjamin	235	244	Pri.	I	8 Md. Inf.	29 Oct. 1862	8 Aug. 1863	
	Fowblesburg, Md.	Sight - hearing						Expiration term service	
15516.	BOSLEY, Levi	236	245	Corpl	G	4 Md. Inf.	11 Aug. 1862	27 June 1864	2 10
	Butler, Md.							Expiration term service	
15517.	AUSTIN, Ferdinand	252	261	Pri.	H	3 Md. Inf.	15 Oct. 1862	3 Aug. 1863	
	Boring, Md.	Prolapsus in arm - deafness						Expiration term service	
15518.	HAUGHEY, Francis	256	266	Pri.	B	11 Md. Inf.	18 Sept. 1864	16 June 1865	
	Woodensbury, Md.	Partial deafness						Expiration term service	
15519.	√HAUGHEY, Francis	256	266	Pri.	B	Tyler Bat.	16 June 1864	18 Sept. 1864	
	Woodensbury, Md.								
15520.	MYERS, Clearfield	262	274	Pri.	E	1 Md. Vet. Cav.	18 Feb. 1864	8 Aug. 1865	
	Boring, Md.	Chronic diarrhoea &c.							
15521.	THOMAS, John	78	79	# note	Line	(remarks)	186	186	
	Glyndon, Md.	Away from home, wife knew nothing more than (U. S. Soldier)							
15522.	BOWERS, Andrew F.	277	290	Pri.	B	8 Md. Inf.	22 Aug. 1862	31 May 1865	
	Glyndon, Md.	Rheumatism							
15523.	*FORTUNE, Thomas	125	127	Sol.			186	186	
	Baltimore, Md.								
15524.	*SELLMAN, Jacob	162	164	Sol.			186	186	
	Baltimore, Md.								

Page No. 1
Supervisor's District No. 1st Md
Enumeration District No. 423

Eleventh Census of the United States

SPECIAL SCHEDULE
SURVIVING SOLDIERS, SAILORS, AND MARINES, AND WIDOWS, ETC.

Persons who served in the Army, Navy, and Marine Corps of the United States during the war of the rebellion (who are survivors), and widows of such persons, in   Reisterstown   County of   Balto   State of   Maryland.   enumerated in June 1890

Jesse M. Harden
Enumerator

	1	2	3	4	5	6	7	8	9 Yrs Mos Dys
15525.	BLIZZARD, John A. Woodensburg			Pri.	B	8 Md.	Augst 14 1862	Feby 1864	60
15526.	AMBROSE, Geo. W. Reisterstown	26 Rhumatism	7	Pri.	C	11 Md.	1st May 1864	Nov. 25 1864 Honorable discharge	6
15527.	(Conf) WAGGONER, Henry E. Reisterstown	28 Shot in left wrist	7	Pri.	D	5th Tenesee	Apl. 1 1861	May 1864	4 1
15528.	BRIHEIM, August Reisterstown	66 Chronic diareah &c.	2	Pri.	B	109 New York	Augt. 1862	1865 Honable discharge	3
15529.	BAKER, John Reisterstown,	63 Rhumatism & hearing effective	3	Pri.	E	165 Penn.	Oct. 16 1863	July 28 1863 Honable discharge	9
15530.	(Conf) CONRAD, Peter M. Reisterstown	104	4	Pri.	F	10 Va. Inft.	May 1861	June 1865	4
15531.	BROWN, Jacob F. H. Reisterstown	132	1	Pri.		1st Md. Homes	1862	1863 Captured and paroled 6th Sept. 63	
15532.	GROVE, John W. (Conf) Reisterstown			Pri.		4th Md. Batery	Jany 1862	186 Captured and taken to Camp Chase	1 6
15533.	(Conf) STANSFIELD, Benjamin L. Reisterstown	153	9	Lieut.	B	3 Maryland	June 3 1862	186	2 6
15534.	LOGUE, James T. Reisterstown	169 Bad health in general incurred	8	Pri.	F	4th Md. Inf.	Augt 11 1862	June 10 1865 Honorable discharge	2 10
15535.	(Conf) ELLISON, Geo. J. Reisterstown	187	6	Pri.	A	4th Va.	Apl 16 1861	July 2 1865	4 4
15536.	NEEL, John A. Reisterstown	193 Hospital 5 months	3	Sergant	B	8th Md.	Aug. 14 1862	May 31 1865 Honorable discharge	2 9 27

Special Schedule. Surviving Soldiers, Sailors, and Marines, and Widows, etc.

Page

S. D.: 1st Md. ; E. D.: 423 ; Minor Civil Division.:

	1	2	3	4	5	6	7	8	9 Yrs Mos Dys
15537.	NORRIS, Wm. (Conf) Reisterstown	244 Wounded in right hand	12	Col.	Chef Sig core		April 1861 Prisoner of war on parole	May 1865	4

15538.	ABNER, James J.	293	4	Pri.	I	111 Ill.	June	1863	186	3
	Glyndon							Waiting for exchange		
15539.	FLEETWOOD, Wm. H.	299	8	Teamster				1861	186	
	Reisterstown	Hospital fever						Captured and taken to hospital		
15540.	GOODWIN, Wm. F.	307		Surgeon				186	186	2	6

Page No. 1
Supervisor's District No. 1
Enumeration District No. 424

Eleventh Census of the United States

SPECIAL SCHEDULE
SURVIVING SOLDIERS, SAILORS, AND MARINES, AND WIDOWS, ETC.

Persons who served in the Army, Navy, and Marine Corps of the United States during the war of the rebellion (who are survivors), and widows of such persons, in   Fifth District   County of   Baltimore
State of   Maryland.   enumerated in June 1890

Frederick S. Myerly
Enumerator

1	2	3	4	5	6	7	8	9		
								Yrs	Mos	Dys
15541. ALDER, John R. (U. S.) Mt. Carmel, Baltimore, Md.	61	62	Private	K	11th	Aug. 10 1862	June 15 1865	3		
15542. BURGOYNE, Henry A. (Conf) Grave Run, Mills, Md.	65	67	Orderly Sergeant	E	Eng Corp.	Sept. 1 1863	April 8 1865	1	7	7
15543. WILHELM, Joshua G. (U. S.) Beckeysville, Baltimore Co., Md.	80	87	Corporal	G	9th Md. Reg.	June 25 1863	Jan. 17 1865	1	6	22
15544. BELL, James Mt. Carmel, Baltimore, Co., Md.	148	153	Private	C	1st Md. Reg.	Nov. 12 1861	Aug. 8 1865	3	8	26
15545. KELBAUGH, Thomas Mt. Carmel, Baltimore Co., Md.	153	158	Private	C	13th Md. Reg.	Jan. 25 1865	June 8 1865		4	15
15546. QUINN, James Butler, Baltimore, Co., Md.	201	208	Private	B	1st Md. Reg.	July 15 1864	July 2 1865		11	13
15547. WALTEMEYER, Adam Mt. Carmel, Baltimore Co., Md.	137	142	Private	G F	12 Pa. Reserves 150 Pa. Buck	Feb. 15 1864 May 1864	July 3 1865	1	4	18
			Lost hearing in left ear and slightly wounded in left foot							
15548. PARKER, James Shamburgh, Baltimore Co., Md.	51	52	Private	I	11th Md. Reg.	Aug. 25 1862	June 15 1865	2	8	16
15549. NACE, John Butler, Baltimore Co., Md.	206	244	Private				186	186		
							He is unable to find his papers			
15550. *SANBLE, John S.	85	87	Sol.				186	186		

Page No. 1
Supervisor's District No. 1
Enumeration District No. 425

Eleventh Census of the United States

SPECIAL SCHEDULE
SURVIVING SOLDIERS, SAILORS, AND MARINES, AND WIDOWS, ETC

Persons who served in the Army, Navy, and Marine Corps of the United States during the war of the rebellion (who are survivors), and widows of such persons, in 3rd District County of Baltimore State of Maryland. enumerated in June 1890

G. A. Ebaugh
Enumerator

	1	2	3	4	5	6	7	8	9 Yrs	Mos	Dys
15551.	RHINAMON, David Hampstead, Carroll Co., Md.	28	28	Private Rheumatism in leg and went through system	K	8 Md. Inft.	29 Oct. 1862	3 Aug. 1863		9	4
15552.	HARE, Jesse Grave Run Mills, Balto., Co., Md.	35	35	Private Gun shot wound in back	C	1 Md. Calv.	29 Feb. 1864	8 Aug. 1865	1	5	9
15553.	FOUBLE, Oliver P. Grave Run Mills, Balto., Co., Md.	51	51	Private Rheumatism fever sore leg	G	4 Md. Inft.	30 Aug. 1862	19 Jan. 1864	1	4	19
15554.	COX, Oliver Black Rock, Balto., Co., Md.	58	58	Corporal Chronic diarrhoea gun shot wound on rt. Foot	I	6 Md. Inft.	14 Aug. 1862	20 June 1865	2	10	6
15555.	WALLET, John Trenton, Balto., Co., Md.	83	84	Private Injured in back by to fall of a horse	F	8 Pa. Calv.	24 Aug. 1861	27 Aug. 1864	3	0	3
15556.	GORDON, James H. Butler, Balto., Co., Md.	102	103	Private Wounded in right shoulder chronic diarrhoea	B	5 M,d. Inft.	Feb. 1864	July 1865	1		17
15557.	HOOVER, George Butler, Balto., Co., Md.	123	124	Private Weak lungs & kidney trouble	K	153 Ind. Inft.	1 Feb. 1865	27 June 1865		4	26
15558.	BOSLEY, John H. Upperco, Balto., Co., Md.	148	149	Private	G	4 Md. Inft.	10 Sept. 1862	31 May 1865	2	8	21
15559.	BOSLEY, William H. Trenton, Balto., Co., Md.	158	159	Private Wounded in arm	G	4 Md. Inft.	10 Sept. 1862	31 May 1865	2	8	21
15560.	BELT, Benjamin F. Boring, Balto., Co., Md.	162	163	Private Erysipelas on nose	Md. Calv. C	Purnell Legion	29 Aug. 1862	31 May 1865	2	9	2
15561.	MYERS, Elisha Boring, Balto., Co., Md.	172	173	Private Rheumatism	I	8 Md. Inft.	29 Oct. 1862	8 Aug. 1863 Now quite poorly		9	9
15562.	GRIMM, William Upperco, Balto., Co., Md.	1 85	187	Corporal	B	166 Pa. Inft.	24 Oct. 1862	28 July 1865		11	4

Special Schedule. Surviving Soldiers, Sailors, and Marines, and Widows, etc.

Page 2   S. D.: 1 ; E. D.: 425 ; Minor Civil Division.: 5th Dist. West of Falls Turnpike

	1	2	3	4	5	6	7	8	9 Yrs	Mos	Dys
15563.	Mary, widow of EBAUGH, Nichola Upperco, Balto., Co., Md.	200	203	Private Wounded in right hip	B	3 Md. Inft.	13 Nov. 1861	4 Jan. 1864	2	1	21
15564.	LEWIS, George A. Upperco, Balto., Co., Md.	202	205	Private Wounded in right hand	M	2 U. S. Col. Calv.	186	186	2	6	
15565.	HAGER, John C. Upperco, Balto., Co., Md.	207	210	Private Slightly wounded in left hip	C	6 Md. Inft.	13 Aug. 1862	24 June 1865	2	10	11
15566.	PRECHTEL, George Upperco, Balto., Co., Md.	208	211	Band & Seargeant	Musician	2 U. S. Art.	1 Sept. 1863	1 Sept. 1868	5	0	0
15567.	CROWTHER, Eli Trenton, Balto., Co., Md.	223	226	Corporal Gun shot wound wrist & left side hearing affected	I	6 Md. Inft.	14 Aug. 1862	20 June 1865	2	10	6
15568.	ADAMS, Samuel Upperco, Balto., Co., Md.	180	182	Private Wounded in left leg & side	B	Oseola 39 Md. Inft.	Mch 1864	Dec. 1865	1	9	
15569.	HILL, Reuben Butler, Balto., Co., Md.	151	152	Private Rheumatism	H	18 Ma. Inft.	1864	1865			

Page No. 1
Supervisor's District No. 1
Enumeration District No. 426

Eleventh Census of the United States

SPECIAL SCHEDULE
SURVIVING SOLDIERS, SAILORS, AND MARINES, AND WIDOWS, ETC

Persons who served in the Army, Navy, and Marine Corps of the United States during the war of the rebellion (who are survivors), and widows of such persons, in Sixth Election District County of Baltimore State of Maryland. enumerated in June 1890

Jacob N. Palmer
Enumerator

	1	2	3	4	5	6	7	8	9 Yrs	Mos	Dys
15570.	BAHN, John C. Stiltz, York Co., Pa.	1 None	1	Corporal	G	20 N. Y. Mil.	19 Apr. 1864	9 July 1865	1	2	20
15571.	Elizabeth, widow of HOFFMAN, Cincinnatti Stiltz, York Co., Pa.	4	4				186	186			
15572.	ROYSTON, Caleb Ekler, Balto., Co., Md.	9	9	Private	D	12 Md. Inf.	23 July 1864	6 Nov. 1864		3	13

No.	Name			Rank	Co.	Regiment	Enlisted	Discharged	Yrs	Mos	Dys
15573.	Sarah, widow of RUHL, William Freeland, Md.	28	30	Private	K	8 Md. Inf.	12 Nov. 1862	15 Aug. 1863		9	3
15574.	WINEHOLDT, George F. New Freedom, Pa.	29	31	Private	K	8 Md. Inf.	11 Nov. 1862	15 Aug. 1863		9	4
15575.	SLENBAKER, John H. Freeland, Md.	50 Shot in right hand	52	Private	I	4 Md. Inf.	22 Aug. 1862	10 June 1865	2	9	19
15576.	WILHELM, Henry Eklo, Md.	83 Bronchitis & hearing	88	Private	F	4 Md. Vol.	29 July 1862	5 Jan. 1863 Now deaf in right ear		5	7
15577.	WILHELM, Henry Eklo, Md.	83	88	2nd Lieut.	F	4 Md. Vol.	5 Jan. 1863	21 Mar. 1864	1	2	16
15578.	√WILHELM, Henry Eklo, Md.	83	88	1st Lieut.	F	4 Md. Vol.	21 Mar. 1864	15 Sep. 1864		5	25
15579.	√WILHELM, Henry Eklo, Md.	83	88	Capt.	A	4 Md. Vol.	15 Sept. 1864	31 May 1865		8	16
15580.	DARR, William Dar., Balto. Co., Md.	88 Diarhea & lumbago	94	Private	I	9 Md. Vol.	30 June 1863	27 Apr. 1864		9	28
15581.	WILHELM, Daniel F. Dar., Balto., Co., Md.	90 Catarrh in head	96	Private			186	186 Discharge for disability papers lost drafted man			

Special Schedule. Surviving Soldiers, Sailors, and Marines, and Widows, etc.

Page 2   S. D.: 1   ; E. D.: 426   ; Minor Civil Division.: Sixth Election District

1	2	3	4	5	6	7	8	9		
								Yrs	Mos	Dys
15582. Victoria V., widow of GUTERMAN, Charles Freeland, Md.	106 Loss of one arm	113	Private		2 U. S. Inf.	9 Aug. 1861	4 Feb. 1864 Discharge on surgeon's certificate	2	5	25
15583. Victoria V., widow of √GUTERMAN, Charles Freeland, Md.	106	113	Private		2nd Bat. Vet. Res. Cav.	21 Feb. 1864	30 Apr. 1866	2	2	3
15584. Victoria V., widow of √GUTERMAN, Charles Freeland, Md.	106	113	Hospital Steward			11 May 1867	29 Oct. 1869	2	5	18
15585. MONROE, William Freeland, Md.	106	113	Private	E	5 Md. Vol.	12 Sept. 1861	31 Dec. 1863	2	3	19
15586. √MONROE, William Freeland, Md.	106	113	Private	E	5 Md. Vol.	1 Jan. 1864	1 Sept. 1865	1	9	0

	1	2	3	4	5	6	7	8	9
15587.	WILHELM, William T. Dar., Balto., Co., Md.	91	97	Private Lumbago	A	11 Md. Inf.	May 1864	Oct. 1864 Papers stolen	4
15588.	Mary C., widow of McCANN, Phinas J. Eklo, Md.	155	163	Private	C	7 Md. Vol.	Sep. 1862	June 1865	2 9
15589.	Mary C., widow of WISEMAN, Grafton E. Bentley Springs, Md.	113	120	Corporal Taken prisoner	I	9 Md. Inf.	186	186 Never returned home	
15590.	COOPER, John Jr. Ecklo, Md.	125	132	Private Chronic rheumatism	I	9 Md. Inf.	29 June 1863	19 Mar. 1864 Prisoner Belle Isle 4 mos 20 da.	9 11
15591.	BULL, Christopher Freeland, Md.	135	142	Private Dysintery & kidney trouble	K	8 Md. Mil.	15 Oct. 1863	15 Jan. 1864	3
15592.	MAGEE, Benjamin Bentley Springs, Md.	139	146	Private	K	8 Md. Mil	29 Oct. 1862	3 Aug. 1863	9 4
15593.	WILHELM, Samuel Bentley Springs, Md.	141	148	Private Rheumatism head & joints	A	11 Md. Vol.	20 May 1864	1 Sep. 1864	3 10
15594.	McCLEARY, Wesley Bentley Springs, Md.	146	153	Private Rheumatism of back	G	12 Pa. Vol.	31 July 1861	11 June 1864	2 10 10
15595.	SCOTT, Harry Rayville, Md.	164	172	Musician	I	133 Pa. Vol.	12 Aug. 1862	20 May 1863	9 8

Special Schedule. Surviving Soldiers, Sailors, and Marines, and Widows, etc.

Page

S. D.:   ; E. D.:   ; Minor Civil Division.:

	1	2	3	4	5	6	7	8	9
									Yrs Mos Dys
15596.	SCOTT, Harry Rayville, Md.	164	179	Musician Contracted scurvy	B	36 Pa. Mil.	June 1863	Sept. 1863 Some of the discharge papers	3
15597.	√ SCOTT, Harry Rayville, Md.	164	179	Private And dyspesia	F	13 Jerrs. Inf	Nov. 1864	25 July 1865 Are lost hence Dates are not eplt.	8
15598.	*GERE, Caroline 6th District	129	136				186	186	

Page No. 1
Supervisor's District No. 1
Enumeration District No. 427

Eleventh Census of the United States

SPECIAL SCHEDULE
SURVIVING SOLDIERS, SAILORS, AND MARINES, AND WIDOWS, ETC

Persons who served in the Army, Navy, and Marine Corps of the United States during the war of the rebellion (who are survivors), and widows of such persons, in   Sixth District   County of   Baltimore
State of   Maryland.   enumerated in June 1890

Chas. E. Fultz

Enumerator

	1	2	3	4	5	6	7	8	9		
									Yrs	Mos	Dys
15599.	EHRHART, Samuel Hoffmanville, Balto., o., Md.	16	20	Private	I	8th Md. Inf.	Oct. 29 1862	8 Aug. 1863	0	9	9
15600.	GRIMM, Daniel Stiltz, York Co., Pa.	17	21 Chronic rheumatism, piles, lumbago & palpitation of heart	Private	K	8th Md. Vol.	Apr. 18 1863	Feb. 5 1864 Treated by Dr. H. W. Fair		9	18
15601.	FRITZ, George Hoffmanville, Balto., Co., Md.	38	42 Piles	Private	E	1st Md. Cav.	Feb. 23 1864	Aug. 8 1865 Unable to work	1	5	15
15602.	STORM, Charles Eklo, Balto., Co., Md.	41	45 Consumption	Private	H	3rd Md. Inf.	Oct. 15 1862	Aug. 5 1863 At present unable to work		9	20
15603.	FULTZ, George M. Mudge, Balto., Co., Md.	80	86 None	1st Sergt.	K	8th Md. Vol.	Oct. 29 1862	Aug. 3 1863		9	4
15604.	Sarah A., widow of NACE, Henry Beckleysville, Balto., Co., Md.	96	104 Heart disease	Private	D	1st Md. Cav.	Nov. 28 1864	Aug. 8 1865 Now dead	1	4	10
15605.	Margaret Baublitz, widow of BAUBLITZ, John Mudge, Balto., Co., Md.	97	105 Ruptured	Private	K	8th Md. Vol.	186	discharge 186 lost Now dead			
15606.	ENSOR, Charles Beckleysville, Balto., Co., Md.	98	106 Nothing	Private		Papers lost	186	186			
15607.	KALP, Henry Hoffmanville, Balto., Co., Md.	114	124	Private	G	4th Md Vol.	Aug. 11 1862	May 31 1864 Had typhoid fever in Army	2	9	20
15608.	BANBLITZ, Daniel Beckleysville, Balto., C., Md.	112	122 Wounded right fore arm at Spottsylvania Court House left hand one finger off	Private	G	4th Md. Vol.	Aug. 22 1862	Jan. 22 1865	2	5	0
15609.	HAILE, Abraham Shamberg, Balto., Co., Md.	136	146 Rheumatism	Private		papers forward to	186	Washington 186 A disabled man			
15610.	KIDD, Lloyd N. Rayville, Balto., Co., Md.	146	156 Rheumatism	Private	I	11 Md. Inf.	Aug. 29 1862	June 15 1864 Paroled prisoner			

Special Schedule. Surviving Soldiers, Sailors, and Marines, and Widows, etc.

Page 2   S. D.: 1   ; E. D.: 427   ; Minor Civil Division.: Part of Sixth District

	1	2	3	4	5	6	7	8	9		
									Yrs	Mos	Dys
15611.	McCOY, Johnny Ekls, Baltio., Co., Md.	160	160 Thrown from horse	Private	I	Potomac Home Brigade	Mar. 14 1864	June 28 1865 Hurt in shoulder	1	3	14

	1	2	3	4	5	6	7	8	9
15612.	NELSON, Daniel S. Raysville, Balto., Co., Md.	162	172	Private Deafness & rheumatism	H	8 Md. Vol.	Oct. 20 1862	July 4 1864	1 8 24
15613.	Julia A. Hunt, widow of HUNT, John W. Rayville, Md.			Private	5	Purnell Legion	186	papers 186 lost	
15614.	TAYLOR, James Eklo, Balto., Co., Md.	173	183				186	186	
15615.	MICHAEL, Jacob O. Eklo, Balto., Co., Md.	184	194	Sergt. Intestinal colic disease of spine	F	2nd Md. V. V.	July 6 1861	July 17 1865 Unable to work	4 0 11
15616.	BAUBLITZ, Samuel Eklo, Balto., Co., Md.	185	195	Private Wounded right breast & shoulder	D	3rd Md. Vol.	Oct. 15 1862	July 15 1863	0 9 0
15617.	KIRK, David Eklo, Balto., Co., Md.	203	213	Private	I	11th Md. Vol.	Aug. 27 1862	June 15 1865	2 10 24
15618.	PARRISH, John Eklo, Balto., Co., Md.	204	215	Private Rupture left testicle	F	4th Md. Vol.	Aug. 7 1862	May 31 1865	2 10 7
15619.	PARRISH, Peter Eklo, Balto., Co., Md.	205	216	Private Disease of throat & back	F	4th Md. Vol.	Aug. 7 1862	May 31 1865	2 10 7
15620.	COOPER, Thomas D. M. Eklo, Balto., Co., Md.	208	219	Drummer	A	9th Md. Vol.	July 9 1862	lost 186	
15621.	PRICE, Ephraim Eklo, Balto., Co., Md.	210	221	Private		deserter	186	186	0 3 0
15622.	Susan, widow of CROSS, Valentine Eklo, Balto., Co., Md.	217	228	Sergt.	K	8th Md. Vol.	Oct. 29 1862	Aug. 3 1863	0 9 4
15623.	HOFFMAN, Peter B. Mudge, Balto., Co., Md.	225	236	Private	I	8th Md. Vol.	Oct. 29 1862	Aug. 8 1863	0 9 9
15624.	ZIEGMAN, William Mudge, Balto., Co., Md.	230	241	Private Bilious & rheumatism	H	1st Vet. Res.	Aug. 1862	July 14 1865 Unable to work hard	2 11 9

Special Schedule. Surviving Soldiers, Sailors, and Marines, and Widows, etc.

S. D.: 1 ; E. D.: 427 ; Minor Civil Division.: Part of sixth District   Page 3

	1	2	3	4	5	6	7	8	Yrs Mos Dys
15625.	BUPP, Henry D. Hoffmanville, Balto., Co., Md.	232	243	Private Ague & dropsy	B	166th Penn. Inf.	Nov. 7 1862	186 Has no discharge	1 0 0
15626.	FLORSTEDT, Frederick Hoffmanville, Balto., Co., Md.	233	244	Private Wounded in head	C	15th N. Y. Art.	Oct. 1 1863	May 17 1865	1 7 17
15627.	BOLLINGER, George Mudge, Balto., Co., Md.	238	249	Private	A	12th Md. Vol.	July 9 1864	Nov. 6 1864	0 3 27

Page No.
Supervisor's District No. 1
Enumeration District No. 428

Eleventh Census of the United States

SPECIAL SCHEDULE
SURVIVING SOLDIERS, SAILORS, AND MARINES, AND WIDOWS, ETC

Persons who served in the Army, Navy, and Marine Corps of the United States during the war of the rebellion (who are survivors), and widows of such persons, in Baltimore County of Baltimore State of Maryland, enumerated in June 1890

Clarence Warfield
Enumerator

1	2	3	4	5	6	7	8	9
								Yrs Mos Dys
15628. SHELTON, William H. (U. S.) 116 S. Patterson Park Ave.	11 Partially blind from bursting of cap	13	Private	K	Home Guard Maryland	186 Chronic pain in jade & hemorrhoids unreadable	186	
15629. THOMPSON, J. Richards (U. S.) 2208 E. Patt St.	28 None	32	Canton Marine		Pilot boat Conquest &	Spring 1864	186	
15630. WILSON, Edward (U. S.) 2206 E. Pratt St.	29 None	30	Lieut.	2nd	Maryland Regiment	186 Don't remember when entered or discharge	186	
Caroline Meyer, wife of 15631. MEYERS, John (U. S.) 2204 E. Pratt St.	Shot in knee		Private			186 Widow knows no more particulars	186	
15632. WILLIAMS, William I. (U. S.) 2202 E. Pratt St.	None		Sargeant			1863 Served about three weeks	1863	
Hester A. MacLea, widow of 15633. MacLEA, Wm. H. (U. S.) 117 S. Collington Ave.	None		Pilot			186 Widow knows no more particulars	1864	
Susan E. Anderson, widow of 15634. ANDERSON, B. F. (U. S.) 115 S. Collington Ave.	Wounded in foot by ball		Private			186 Widow knows no more particulars	1863	
15635. GATHRIE, John A. (U. S.) 105 S. Collington Ave.	None		Oiler		Hercules and Jackson	1861	1864	3
15636. HOAKER, Benjamin F. (U. S.) 110 S. Collington Ave.	None		Private	I	3rd Maryland Regiment	186	186	
15637. EULAR, Jacob (U. S.) 116 S. Collington Ave.	None		Private	C	6th Maryland Regiment	1862	1864	2
15638. TODD, Samuel (U. S.) 122 S. Collington Ave.	None		Marine			186 Wife knows no more particulars husband Army	186	

15639. RICHARDSON, William H. (U. S.) 222 E. Pratt St.			Private Wounded in side (slight)		Metropohtam Regiment		1861	1864	3

Special Schedule. Surviving Soldiers, Sailors, and Marines, and Widows, etc.

Page

S. D.: ; E. D.: ; Minor Civil Division.:

1	2	3	4	5	6	7	8	9
								Yrs Mos Dys
15640. MORRISON, James H. (U. S.) 2104 E. Pratt St.		None	Marine		Brooklyn		1861	1864	3
15641. MacCLEMENTS, G. Peter (U. S.) 123 Chester St.		None	Sargant		Heavy Artillery 8th Mass. Volunteer		1863	1864	1
Sarah E., Andrews, widow of 15642. ANDREWS, Wm. (U. S.) 119 Chester St.		None	Private				186 Widow away from home and daughter remembr unreadable step fathers name	186	
15643. BUMP, Jesse E. (U. S.) 118 S. Chester St.		None	Private		119 Penna. Regiment		1861	1864	3
15644. PAFF, John J. (U. S.) 122 S. Chester St.		None	Marine		Simr. MacKinad		1863	1864	1
15645. WYATT, Lemuel C. (U. S.) 124 S. Chester St.		None	Marine		Stme. Dawn		186	186	
Tammy Bush, widow of 15646. BUSH, John (Conf) 2032 E. Pratt St.		None	Private				186 Widow has lost all records	186	
15647. *TAYLOR, William B. 114 So. Collington Ave.	55	57	U. S. So				186	186	
15648. *McCOUBRAY, William R. 2116 E. Pratt St.	65	69	U. S. So				186	186	
15649. *MULLEN, Patrick 2116 E. Pratt St.	65	69					186	186	

Page No.
Supervisor's District No. 1
Enumeration District No. 428

Eleventh Census of the United States

SPECIAL SCHEDULE
SURVIVING SOLDIERS, SAILORS, AND MARINES, AND WIDOWS, ETC

Persons who served in the Army, Navy, and Marine Corps of the United States during the war of the rebellion (who are survivors), and widows of such persons, in   Baltimore   County of   Baltimore   ,
State of   Maryland.   enumerated in June 1890

Clarence Warfield
Enumerator

	1	2	3	4	5	6	7	8	9 Yrs	Mos	Dys
15650.	CHALFANT, George F. Md Line, Md.	28	28 Rheumatism	Private	D	195 Pa. Inf.	Feb. 10 1865	Feb. 1 1866		11	20
15651.	SPICER, John W. Bentley Springs, Md.	38	39 Bronchitis, result of small pox	Private	F	Pernell Legion	Sep. 15 1861	Feb. 9 1863	1	4	9
15652.	DEFENDARFER, Solomon Parkton, Balto., Co., Md.	50	51 Chronic rheumatism of back	Corporal	E	2 Md. Inf.	Aug. 29 1862	June 15 1865 Anderson prison 10 mo.	2	9	14
15653.	TAYLOR, James C. Shane, Balto., Co., Md.	54	55 Nervous rheumatism 20 years	Private			186	186 Deserter			
15654.	SIMMS, James W. Shane, Balto., Co., Md.	59	60 Nervous rheumatism 20 years	Private	H	Inf. 7 Md. Vol.	Aug. 22 1862	June 23 1865	2	10	1
15655.	OPINSHAW, Wesley W. Shane, Balto., Co., Md.	60	61	Private	I	2 Md. Inf.	Feb. 19 1864	June 15 1865	1	3	27
15656.	WILLIAMS, John Md Line, Balto., Co., Md.	93	95	Private	I	8 Md. Inf.	Nov. 5 1862	Aug. 27 1863		9	22
15657.	TAYLOR, Isaac Freeland, Balto., Co., Md.	98	100				186	186 Could not obtain the information not at home			
15658.	GORDON, James R. Gorsuch Mills, Baltimore Co., Md.	132	135	Private	D	87 Pa. Inf.	Sep. 27 1861	186 Deserter			
15659.	BAKER, Isaac C. Gorsuch Mills, Baltimore Co., Md.	143	146	Private	A	Inf. 22 Pa. Vol.	Sep. 22 1862	Oct. 10 1862			18
15660.	SMITH, Jacob Gorsuch Mills, Baltimore Co., Md.	144	147 Rheumatism legs, arms and back 25 years	Private	C	Vol. Inf. 39 Md. Col.	Mar. 29 1864	Dec. 4 1865	1	8	5
15661.	GIBBS, Joseph Gorsuch Mills, Baltimore Co., Md.	147	150	Inf. Private	C	130 Pa. Vol.	Aug. 26 1862	May 21 1863		8	25

Special Schedule. Surviving Soldiers, Sailors, and Marines, and Widows, etc.

Page

S. D.: ; E. D.: ; Minor Civil Division.:

1	2	3	4	5	6	7	8	9
								Yrs Mos Dys

	1	2	3	4	5	6	7	8	9		
15662.	SCOTT, William S. Shane, Balto., Co., Md.	159	162 Bullet wound leg	Private	B	39 Pa. Inf.		186 Could not obtain further information not at home	186		
15663.	SHAEFFER, Joseph E. Trump, Balto., Co., Md.	161	164 Bullet wound eye and throat, catarrh	Private	G	Reserve 12 Pa. Inf.	July 31 1861	June 11 1864	2	10	11
15664.	HERSEY, Joseph S. Gorsuch Mills, Balto., Co., Md.	165	168 Rheumatism	Private	C	Potomac Home Brigade 1 Md. Inf.	Feb. 26 1864	May 29 1865 After the Battle of Gettysburg the regiment was reorganized into 13th Md. Inf.	1	3	3
15665.	ZEIGLER, Francis Trump, Balto., Co., Md.	170	173	Private	C	77 Ohio Inf.	1863 Does not know the dates	186			
15666.	CASKEY, John F. Md Line, Balto., Co., Md.	182	185	Private	C	7 Md. Inf	186 Could not obtain the dates	186			
15667.	Hyantha C., widow of SEITZ, Nicholas Maryland Line	200	206	Private			186	186 Was not at home when dwelling was visited			
15668.	FREELAND, Alfred Maryland Line	208	214	Private	H	8 Md. Inf.	Nov. 7 1862	Aug. 27 1863		9	20
15669.	EDIE, John E. Shane	234	240 Minnie ball right hand and right leg	Private	C	87 Pa. Inf.	Sep. 2 1861	Oct. 25 1864	3	1	23
15670.	SIMMS, Thomas A. Trump	209	215 Rheumatism liver & kidney disease 26 yrs	Private	F	11 Md. Inf.	June 16 1864	Sep. 30 1864		3	14

Page No. 1
Supervisor's District No. 1
Enumeration District No. 429

Eleventh Census of the United States

SPECIAL SCHEDULE
SURVIVING SOLDIERS, SAILORS, AND MARINES, AND WIDOWS, ETC.

Persons who served in the Army, Navy, and Marine Corps of the United States during the war of the rebellion (who are survivors), and widows of such persons, in   S. ½ 2nd Precinct, 7th District   County of   Baltimore   ,
State of   Maryland.   enumerated in June 1890

John S. McGirr
Enumerator

	1	2	3	4	5	6	7	8	9		
									Yrs	Mos	Dys
15671.	HARRIS, Joshua L. Hereford, Md.	39	66	Private	E	Burney's No. Corps 40 No record of dates	Jan. 18 1864	Apr. 1 1865	0	3 or 4	0
15672.	FOARD, William McK. Hereford, Md.	58	65	Private	H	32 Penn's.	June 1864	186	3	0	0
15673.	HOPKINS, William F. Hereford, Md.	45	49	Private		Alleghany	Mar. 12 1863	Sept. 5 1864	1	6	3

No.	Name			Rank	Co.	Regiment	Enlisted	Discharged	Yrs	Mos	Dys
15674.	HUNT, George O. Hereford, Md.	42	46	Private	E	2 Md. Inf.	Aug. 28 1862	Oct. 28 1865	3	2	0
15675.	GILL, Joshua Hereford, Md.	48	55	Private	F	2 Md. Inf.	Dec. 1 1861	July 25 1865	3	1	28
15676.	Sarah Gole, wife of CASWELL, Charles Monkton, Md.	52	61	Private	E	8 Mass. Inf.	1862	1865 Cannot recall dates	3	3	0
15677.	BOND, James D. Monkton, Md.	58 Eyes injured	65	Private	C	39th Md. Inf.	Nov. 24 1862	Dec. 4 1865	3	0	0
15678.	HICKS, John W. Glencoe, Md.	75	81	Private	I	11th Md. Inf.	Apr. 21 1862	June 19 1865	2	10	0
15679.	COX, John Monkton, Md.	83	89	Private	H	32 Pa. Inf.	Feb. 10 1864	Aug. 1865	1		
15680.	HARRIS, John W. Monkton, Md.	59	66	Private	F	39th Md. Inf.	Mar. 1862	Oct. 1863	1	7	0
15681.	MITCHELL, Alexander R. M.D. Hereford, Md.	83	89	Cadet Midshipman		Santee & Constitution	June 8 1872	Apr. 30 1874	1	10	22
15682.	DORSEY, James H. Monkton, Md.	12	13	Cook		Winnepeg Flook	1865	1867	1	6	0

Special Schedule. Surviving Soldiers, Sailors, and Marines, and Widows, etc.

Page 2   S. D.: 1   ; E. D.: 429   ; Minor Civil Division.: S. ½ s Precinct, 7th District

	1	2	3	4	5	6	7	8	9		
									Yrs	Mos	Dys
15683.	CARMAN, Arthur S. Hereford, Balto., Co., Md.	90	96	Private	A	21 Pa. Cav.	Feb. 28 1863	July 28 1865	2	4	0
15684.	John Mayes, alias MAYES, John T. Hereford, Balto., Co., Md.	100	106	Private Dyspepsia & malarial fever	C	1st P. H. B. Inf.	June 15 1862	May 29 1865	2	11	0
15685.	Nicholas Mayes, alias MAYES, Nicholas F. Hereford, Balto., Co., Md.	103	108	Private	G	1st Md. Inf.	May 17 1761	May 23 1864	3	0	0
15686.	FREDERICK, Nelson Parkton, Balto., Co., Md.	108	114	Private	G	4th Md. Inf.	Aug. 18 1862	July 11 1865 Wounded in hip & thigh - no disability	2	10	23
15687.	THOMPSON, Thomas Evna, Balto., Co., Md.	128	134	Corporal	I	2nd E. S. Md.	Sept. 18 1862	June 25 1865	2	9	15

15688.	William I. Scott, alias NICOLL, William J. Hereford, Balto., Co., Md.	134	139	Private	G	2nd Md. Inf.	With Hab. Cor. Mar. 1861 Retired on (at instance of Father) writ of habeas corpus	186			
15689.	William I. Scott, alias √NICOLL, William J. Hereford, Balto., Co., Md.	134	139	2nd Lieutenant	H	Detached	1863	July 1865	0	7	7
15690.	DIRSCHNER, John C. Hereford, Balto., Co., Md.	136	141	Private	D	4 Md. Inf.	Mar. 7 1862	May 26 1862	0	2	27
15691.	√DIRSCHNER, John C. Hereford, Balto., Co., Md.	136	141	Corporal	H	10 Md. Inf.	June 23 1863	Jan. 29 1864	0	7	7
15692.	SCHULTZ, Amos Hereford, Balto., Co., Md.	137	142		H	8th Md. Inf.	Nov. 3 1862	Aug. 27 1863	0	9	24
15693.	MARTIN, Charles I. Evna, Balto., Co., Md.	140	145	Private	D	7th Md. Inf.	Aug. 15 1862	Jan. 9 1865			
15694.	√MARTIN, Charles I. Evna, Balto., Co., Md.	140	145	Corporal	D	7th Md. Inf.	Aug. 15 1862	Jan. 9 1865	2	10	24

Page No. 1
Supervisor's District No. 1
Enumeration District No. 430

Eleventh Census of the United States

SPECIAL SCHEDULE
SURVIVING SOLDIERS, SAILORS, AND MARINES, AND WIDOWS, ETC.

Persons who served in the Army, Navy, and Marine Corps of the United States during the war of the rebellion (who are survivors), and widows of such persons, in 7th District County of Baltimore State of Maryland. enumerated in June 1890

William L. Markland
Enumerator

	1	2	3	4	5	6	7	8	9 Yrs	Mos	Dys
15695.	BULL, Joshua L. Parkton, Balto., Co., Md.	26	26 Rheumatism	Corporal	I	9 Md. Reg.	Jan. 29 1863	June 20 1864	8	9	21
15696.	Lavina, widow of ROACHE, Jessie Parkton, Balto., Co., Md.	27	27 Throat & lungs diseased	Private			186	186 Unable to work			
15697.	COOPER, William T. Parkton, Balto., Co., Md.	28	28 Rhumatism & hearing	Private	G	4 Md. Reg.	Aug. 30 1862	May 31 1865	2	9	1
15698.	STIFFLER, William H. Parkton, Balto., Co., Md.	19	19 Rheumatism	Private	G	4 Md. Reg.	Aug. 14 1862	May 25 1865	2	9	11
15699.	THOMAS, John H. Rayville, Balto., Co., Md.	11	11 Ague & heart disease	Corporal	H	6 U. S. Vol.	Aug. 24 1863	Sep. 20 1865 Unable to work	2	0	26
15700.	MASEMORE, George H. Rayville, Balto., Co., Md.	31	32 Piles & diarrhea	Corporal	I	8 Md. Reg.	Oct. 15 1862	Aug. 10 1863	0	9	25

		1	2	3	4	5	6	7	8	9		
15701.	BAKER, Henry F. Parkton, Balto., Co., Md.	38	39		Private	I	11 Md. Reg.	Aug. 30 1862	June 15 1865	2	9	16
15702.	BALL, Eli. S. Parkton, Balto., Co., Md.	47	48		Private	F	1 Md. Vol.	Jan. 6 1862	July 2 1865	3	0	26
15703.	MARTIN, Eli Parkton, Balto., Co., Md.	73	74		Private Heart disease	F	3 Md. Reg.	186	186			
15704.	SHAW, Silas H. Parkton, Balto., Co., Md.	86	87		Private	B	56 Pa. Reg.	Oct. 4 1864	July 1 1865	0	8	27
15705.	PRICE, John S. Parkton, Balto., Co., Md.	82	83		Consg.		2 Md. Reg.	186	186			
15706.	JONES, Aaron Parkton, Balto., Co., Md.	80	81		Private Rheumatism	G	30 Md. Reg.	1863	1864	1	0	0

Special Schedule. Surviving Soldiers, Sailors, and Marines, and Widows, etc.

Page

S. D.: ; E. D.: ; Minor Civil Division.:

		1	2	3	4	5	6	7	8	9		
										Yrs	Mos	Dys
15707.	KITE, John H. White Hall, Balto., Co., Md.	94	95		Private	H	9 Md. Reg.	July 28 1863	Feb. 23 1864	0	6	28
15708.	BURNS, John T. White Hall, Balto., Co., Md.	89	90		Private	H	8 Md. Reg.	1862	1863	1	0	0
15709.	KEECH, James O. White Hall, Balto., Co., Md.	95	96		Private	A	Prnl. Leg. Md.	Nov. 7 1861	Nov. 27 1864	3	0	20
15710.	STARKS, C. M. Calvert Station, Baltimore	62	63		1st Srg. Shot through leg & diarrhoea	H	18 U. S. Inft.	July 14 1862	July 14 1865	3	0	0
15711.	BURNS, Richard N. White Hall, Balto., Co., Md.	104	105		Corp.	I	9 Md. Reg.	Jan. 29 1863	Feb. 23 1864	0	7	24
15712.	MERRYMAN, W. H. White Hall, Balto., Co., Md.	108	109	Leg mashed	Private	I	11 Md. Inft.	Feb. 23 1864	June 16 1865	2	3	23
15713.	Margaret, widow of FITZGERALD, John D. White Hall, Balto., Co., Md.	122	125		Private	F	Prnl. Leg. Md. Vol.	1861	1864	3	0	0
15714.	LEAGUE, William F. White Hall, Balto., Co., Md.	124	125		Private			1861	1864	3	0	0
15715.	JOHNSON, William H. White Hall, Balto., Co., Md.	123	124		Corp.	I	9 Md. Reg.	Jan. 29 1863	Mar. 20 1864	1	0	21
15716.	CLARK, Henry White Hall, Balto., Co., Md.	109	110		Private	E	27 Vir. Inft.	June 1861	June 1864	3	0	0

	1	2	3	4	5	6	7	8	9		
15717.	JOHNSON, James White Hall, Balto., Co., Md.	128	124	Private	B	M. H. Bat.	July 1863	July 1865	2	0	0
15718.	KING, Michael White Hall, Balto., Co., Md.	199	200	Private	I	9 Md. Reg.	June 29 1863	Mar. 17 1864	0	8	18
15719.	STABLER, Henry H Stablerville, Balto., Co., Md.	163	164	Serg.	K	8 Md. Reg.	Oct. 29 1862	Aug. 3 1863	0	9	4
15720.	BAILEY, Frederick A.	178	174			Pawnee of war	July 12 1864	July 12 1865	1	0	0

Special Schedule. Surviving Soldiers, Sailors, and Marines, and Widows, etc.

Page

S. D.:   1   ; E. D.:   430   ; Minor Civil Division.:

	1	2	3	4	5	6	7	8	9		
									Yrs	Mos	Dys
15721.	KIRKWOOD, Joseph Shanes, Balto., Co., Md.	170	171	Private	H	8 Md. Reg.	Nov. 1 1862	Aug. 27 1863	0	9	26
15722.	WILSON, Edwin Shanes, Balto., Co., Md.	167	168	Private	H	8 Md. Reg.	186	186			
15723.	WRIGHT, John W. Stablersville, Balto., Co., Md.	168	166 Hearing	Private	E	1 Va. Cav.	1861	1865	4	0	0
15724.	BREWER, Charles Shanes, Balto., Co., Md.	148	149 Shot in back	Private	D	9 Pa. Reg.	Mar 1862	July 1865	2	4	0
15725.	WILLIAMS, Charles J. Shanes, Balto., Co., Md.	149	150 Hearing	Private	G	4 Md. Reg.	1862	1865	3	0	0
15726.	TALBOTT, Jeremiah E. Stablersville, Balto., Co., Md.	181	182 Diarrhoea	Private	G	184 Pa. Reg.	1863	1865	2	0	0
15727.	THOMAS, David N. Commills, Balto., Co., Md.	137	138	Private	I	87 Pa. Vol.	Aug. 27 1861	Dec. 1 1863	2	3	4
15728.	(Conf) CAMERON, George H. Walkers Switch, Balto., Co., Md.	219	220	Private	Bethds. Bat.	Lynchburg Bauregard	July 25 1864	Apr. 9 1865	0	10	0
15729.	GALLION, Stansbury Walkers Switch, Balto., Co., Md.	218	219 Shot in thigh	Private	F	2 Md. Vol.	Oct. 12 1861	Dec. 1 1862	1	1	19
15730.	CAMERON, John M. Walkers Switch, Balto., Co., Md.	216	217				186	186			

Special Schedule. Surviving Soldiers, Sailors, and Marines, and Widows, etc.

Page

S. D.:   ; E. D.:   ; Minor Civil Division.:

	1	2	3	4	5	6	7	8	9		
									Yrs	Mos	Dys
15731.	*BAUBLITZ, George Baltimore Co., Md.	35	36				186	186			
15732.	*McNEAL, Rachel B. White Hall, Balto., Co., Md.	104	105				186	186			

Note:-The provision of the act of March 1, 1889, under which this special enumeration of survivors of the war of the rebellion is made, reads as follows:

That said Superintendent shall under the authority of the Secretary of the Interior, cause to be taken on a special schedule of inquiry, according to such form as he may prescribe, the names, organizations, and length of service of those who had served in the Army, Navy, or Marines Corps of the United States in the war of the rebellion, and who are survivors at the time of said inquiry, and the widows of soldiers, sailors, or marines.

The entries concerning each survivor or widow should be carefully and accurately made, so that the printed reports may contain only thoroughly trustworthy information.

Spaces are provided on this special schedule for the entry of fifty names, or more properly, term of service. The spaces are numbered consecutively from 1 to 50, and cover the four pages comprised in each schedule. The inquiries made concerning each survivor or widow call for the repetition of the number of the house and family as returned on the general population schedule (No. 1), the name, rank company, regiment or vessel, date of enlistment, date of discharge, and length of service (in years, months, and days) on the upper half of each page, and the post-office address, disability incurred, and general remarks on the lower half of each page. The column headed "Remarks" is intended to be used to cover any points not included in the forgoing inquires, and which are necessary to a complete statement of a person's term of service in any one organization.

In the case of persons having served in more than one organization, use as many spaces as may be necessary to cover their various terms of service. In the case of widows of deceased soldiers, sailors, or marines, make the entry of her name on the dotted lines, as follows: Mary J., widow of filling out the record of his service during the war, and giving under "post-office address" the Present address of his widow.   BROWN, James H.

Page No.   1
Supervisor's District No. 1
Enumeration District No. 431

Eleventh Census of the United States

SPECIAL SCHEDULE
SURVIVING SOLDIERS, SAILORS, AND MARINES, AND WIDOWS, ETC.

Persons who served in the Army, Navy, and Marine Corps of the United States during the war of the rebellion (who are survivors), and widows of such persons, in   1st Precinct 8th District   County of   Baltimore   ,
State of   Maryland.   enumerated in June 1890

Charles Worthington
Enumerator

	1	2	3	4	5	6	7	8	9		
									Yrs	Mos	Dys
15733.	MERRYMAN, Thomas H. Glencor, Balto., Co., Md.	10	10	Private	D	7 Md. Inf.	14 Aug. 1862	31 May 1865	2	8	17
15734.	Lydia A. Eaton, formerly widow of MORGAN, Thomas Glencor, Balto., Co., Md.	14	15	Private Wounded in the arm	D	2 Md. Inf.	1861	1865			
15735.	PROSSER, Charles S. Corbett, Balto., Co., MD.	26	27	Private	B	21 Pa. Cal.	16 June 1863	17 July 1865	2		1
15736.	MILLER, John W. Corbett, Balto., Co., Md.	34	35	Private	C	1 Md. Inf.	2 May 1861	9 July 1865	4	2	7

	1	2	3	4	5	6	7	8	9		
15737.	Harriet Cortron, widow of CORTRON, James Philopolis, Balto., Co., Md.	45	49 Killed at Petersburg Va.	Private	D	43 U. S. C. T. Vol.	186	186			
15738.	COX, William H. Belfast, Balto., Co., Md.	80	84 Wounded in thigh	Private	D	7 Md. Inf.	14 Aug. 1862	31 May 1865	2	9	17
15739.	GORSUCH, John C. Belfast, Balto., Co., Md.	84	88 Wounded in body	Private	G	1 Md. Inf.	27 Aug. 1862	32 June 1865	2	9	7
15740.	STEWART, Joel Belfast, Balto., Co., Md.	89	93	Private	I E	11 Md. Inf. 2 Md. Inf.	5 Aug. 1862	2 June 1865	2	9	29
15741.	MEYERS, Alfred Belfast, Balto., Co., Md.	106	110	Private	E	Vol. 3 U. S. C. T.	16 Dec. 1864	31 Oct. 1865		10	15
15742.	ILER, John W. Hestern Run, Balto., Co., Md.	143	148	Private	E	Vol. 32 U. S. C. T.	19 Feb. 1864	22 Aug. 1865	1	7	3
15743.	RINGGOLD, Charles Philopolis, Balto., Co., Md.	163	168 Wounded in fingers,	Private	C	Vol. 32 U. S. C. T.	19 Feb. 1864	22 Aug. 1865	1	7	3
15744.	SMITH, Thomas Philopolis, Balto., Co., Md.	164	169	Private	K	114 U. S. C. T. Vol.	186	186			

Special Schedule. Surviving Soldiers, Sailors, and Marines, and Widows, etc.

Page 1   S. D.: 1 ; E. D.: 431   ; Minor Civil Division.: 1st Precinct 8th District

	1	2	3	4	5	6	7	8	9		
									Yrs	Mos	Dys
15745.	POWELL, Isaac Philopolis, Balto., Co., Md.	165	170	Corporal	C	32 U. S. C. Troops	19 Feb 1864	22 Aug. 1865	1	7	3
15746.	NORRIS, Thomas Philopolis, Balto., Co., Md.	161	166	Private	A	drafted 30 U. S. C. T.	13 Jan. 1864	16 June 1865	1	5	3
15747.	TRACEY, Thomas Cockeysville, Balto., Co., Md.	169	174	Private	C	1 Md. Inf.	12 Nov. 1861	12 Nov. 1864	3		
15748.	Rebecca, widow of FITZ, James L. Cockeysville, Balto., Co., Md.	180	185	Private	B	3rd Md. Cal.	1862	1865			
15749.	FRANKLIN, Walter S. Ashland, Balto., Co., Md.	190	195	Colonel	H	12 U. S. Inf.	14 May 1861	resigned 1 Oct. 1870	8	7	26

15750.	RILEY, John L. Ashland, Balto., Co., Md.	203	208	Sargent	E	2 Md. E. S. Inf.	21 Aug. 1862	15 Jan. 1865	2	9	25
15751.	HANSON, Samuel Ashland, Balto., Co., Md.	211	216	Corporal	F	1 Md. Cal.	9 Oct. 1861	20 Dec. 1863	2	2	11
15752.	Rebecca, widow of LEARD, Corbin Ashland, Balto., Co., Md.	212	217 Died at Andersonville	Private	F	1 Md. Cal.	186	186			
15753.	CORTRON, Joseph Philopolis, Balto., Co., Md.	232	237	Private	G	4 U. S. C. T. Inf.	11 Aug. 1863	May 1866	2	8	
15754.	JAMERSON, James H. Philopolis, Balto., Co., Md.	233	238	Sargent	A	39 U. S. C. T. Inf.	21 Mar. 1865	4 Dec. 1866	1	8	13
15755.	Isabella, widow of USEN, William Cockeysville, Balto., Co., Md.	237	242	Private	H	4 U. S. C. T. Inf.	11 Aug. 1863	186			
15756.	RECKLER, Charles Phoenix, Balto. Co., Md.	245	250 Lost sight of left eye	Wagoner	B	81 Pa. Inf.	28 June 1861	13 Dec. 1862	1	6	15
15757.	STEWART, Charles W. Philopolis, Balto., Co., Md.	261	Sailor Ship 268	Waiter		U. S. Custer	10 Feb. 1865 Transferred from U. S. Custer to U. S. Florida	13 Apr. 1867	2	2	13
15758.	TUCKSON, Frederick Philopolis, Balto., Co., Md.	236	241	Private	G	4th U. S. C. T. Inf.	186 Discharge papers lost	186			

Page No. 1
Supervisor's District No. 1
Enumeration District No. 432

Eleventh Census of the United States

SPECIAL SCHEDULE
SURVIVING SOLDIERS, SAILORS, AND MARINES, AND WIDOWS, ETC.

Persons who served in the Army, Navy, and Marine Corps of the United States during the war of the rebellion (who are survivors), and widows of such persons, in 8th District 1st Precinct County of Baltimore
State of Maryland. enumerated in June 1890

W. W. Cullum Stewart
Enumerator

	1	2	3	4	5	6	7	8	9
									Yrs Mos Dys
15759.	KITE, Daniel W. Kite, Daniel Phoenix	3 Rheumatism	3	Private	F	2 Md. Inf.	22 July 1861 Now is crippled in feet, has one arm (left)	17 July 1865	3 11 15
15760.	PRICE, Daniel Price, Daniel Phoenix	8	8	Private	A		Oct. 1863 With Capt. Shriver, when in service	186	about 3
15761.	Elizabeth,, widow FOWLER, James Fowler, Elizabeth Ashland	21	21 Husband was killed in Army	Private	D	7 Md. Inf.	Sept. 1862	186	about 3

Page -45-

No.	Name			Rank	Co.	Regiment	Enlisted	Discharged	Yrs	Mos	Dys
15762.	BUCHANAN, Nathan (col) Buchanan, Nathan (col) Cockeysville	62	65	Private	F	4 Md. inf.	4 Aug. 1863 Discharged	4 May 1866	2	9	0
15763.	ROY, (or ROHE) John Rohe or Roy, John Cockeysville	78	82	Private	M	5 Artillery	16 Apr. 1866 Died June 1st 1890	16 Apr. 1869	3	0	0
15764.	COLE, Jacob (col) Cole, Jacob (col) Cockeysville	66	69	Private	H	29 Ill. Inf.	186 Discharged papers not at home walks lame for 20 yrs	186	1	2	0
15765.	Gorsuch Amelia, widow GORSUCH, Thomas Gorsuch, Amelia Cockeysville	89	94	Private	B	11 Md. Inf.	10 Sept. 1864	15 June 1865	0	9	5
15766.	MORFOOT, Robert Morfoot, Robert Cockeysville	89	94	Corporal Chronic rheumatism & rupture	D	7 Md. Inf.	20 Aug. 1862 Has surgeons discharge	26 July 1865	2	11	6
15767.	MILLER, George W. Miller, George W. Warren	93	98	Private	G	1 Md. Inf.	27 Aug. 1861 Reenlisted veteran	2 July 1865	4	1	5
15768.	GREEN, John W. Green, John W. Cockeysville	95	100	Private	G	1 Md. Inf.	27 May 1861 Discharged	23 May 1864	2	11	26
15769.	DOERR, Henry Doerr, John W. Warren	100	105	Private Struck by shell in the back	E	3 U. S. Inf.	28 Dec. 1861 Reenlisted veteran	31 July 1865	3	7	3
15770.	PURVIANCE, Daniel (col) Purviance, Daniel Warren	108	113	Private	D	38 Va. Inf.	1863	Mar. 1866	3	about	

Special Schedule. Surviving Soldiers, Sailors, and Marines, and Widows, etc.

Page 2   S. D.:   ; E. D.:   ; Minor Civil Division.:

	1	2	3	4	5	6	7	8	9		
									Yrs	Mos	Dys
15771.	HOWARD, Benjamin Warren	120	125	Private	D	7 Md. Inf.	20 Aug. 1862 Discharged	June 1865	2	9	18
15772.	CULLEN, James C. Warren	123	128	Private			186 Was in Government service after the close of late war, per information service recorded his name	186			
15773.	Sarah E., widow of TAYLOR, John H. Warren	126	131	Private	D	7 Md. Inf.	20 Aug. 1862	30 May 1865	2	9	10
15774.	LYNCH, Jethro Warren	128	133	Private Injury to right ankle	G	1 Md. Inf.	3 May 1861	28 Nov. 1864 Now unable to work reenlisted	3	6	25
15775.	UHLER, William H. Warren	134	139	Sergeant Gun shot wound right leg	G	1 Md. Inf.	27 May 1861 Veteran discharged	11 Dec. 1862	1	6	14
15776.	WEAVER, Daniel Warren	160	165	Sergeant	G	1 Md. Inf.	27 May 1861 Reenlisted veteran	2 July 1865	4	1	15

No.	Name				Rank	Co.	Regiment	Enlisted	Discharged	Yrs	Mos	Dys
15777.	STOCKSDON, Franklin (Andrew Haines alias) Warren	161	166		Corporal	F	165 Pa. Inf.	16 Oct. 1862	28 July 1863 Discharged	0	10	12
15778.	HILES, Edmond Warren	164	169		Private Hernia or ruptured in service	K	Conn 18 Con. Inf	13 Aug. 1862	2 June 1865 Now unable to do regular work, discharged	2	9	19
15779.	HOFFMAN, Daniel Warren	181	186		Private	G	1 Md. Inf.	1861	1864			
15780.	FORD, William H. Warren	181	191		Corporal	G	1 Md. Inf.	20 Sept. 1861	27 Feb. 1864 Reenlisted veteran	2	5	7
15781.	BERRY, George (col) Cockeysville	88	93		Corporal	C	30 U. S. Col Troops Inf.	24 Feb. 1864	10 Dec. 1865 Discharged	1	9	16
15782.	SINGLETON, William H. Warren	156	161		Private when he enlisted 2nd Sergeant	H	2 Md. Inf.	13 Aug. 1862	20 July 1865 Discharged	2	11	15
15783.	WILLIAMS, Jacob Warren	168	173		Private	G	1 Md. Inf.	8 Nov. 1861	20 Sept. 1865 Discharged	3	10	12
15784.	THRONGH, William Warren	202	207		Private	K	8 Md. Inf.	29 Oct. 1862	3 Aug. 1863 Discharged	0	9	4

Special Schedule. Surviving Soldiers, Sailors, and Marines, and Widows, etc.

Page

S. D.:   ; E. D.:   ; Minor Civil Division.:

	1	2	3	4	5	6	7	8	9
									Yrs Mos Dys
15785.	SMITH, Robert S. Warren	214	220	Captain	G	1 Md. Inf.	May 1861	1862 Prisoner at Fort Royal, resigned in 62, after being paroled	1 8

Eleventh Census of the United States

Page No.
Supervisor's District No. 1
Enumeration District No. 433

SPECIAL SCHEDULE
SURVIVING SOLDIERS, SAILORS, AND MARINES, AND WIDOWS, ETC

Persons who served in the Army, Navy, and Marine Corps of the United States during the war of the rebellion (who are survivors), and widows of such persons, in   8th Dist, 1st Precinct   County of   Baltimore   ,
State of   Maryland.   enumerated in June 1890

Chas. M. Chilcoat
Enumerator

1	2	3	4	5	6	7	8	9
								Yrs Mos Dys

		1	2	3	4	5	6	7	8	9		
	15786.	ADAMS, Jacob Vinia Adams, widow of Cockeysville, Balto., Co., Md.	24	25	Private	A		186	186			
	15787.	WELSH, Daniel Cockeysville, Balto., Co., Md.	28	29	Private Head affected	I	7 Md. Inf.	18 June 1863 At Petersburg artillery fire	2 July 1865	2	0	14
	15788.	CLARK, William H. Cockeysville, Balto., Co., Md.	38	39	Private Weak back	H	201 Pa. Inf.	20 Aug. 1864	22 June 1865		10	21
June 4	15789.	SCOTT, Abraham Cockeysville, Balto., Co., Md.	45	46	Private Hip out of place			1862 He has no papers	1865			
	15790.	ROBECK, Charles Cockeysville, Balto., Co., Md.	46	47	Private			186 He has no papers	186			
June 5	15791.	ROBINSON, John Cockeysville, Balto., Co., Md.	55	56	Teamster			186 He has no papers	186			
	15792.	COLBERT, Samuel Cockeysville, Balto., Co., Md.	75	78	Private Heart disease	K	13 Md. Inf.	18 Sept. 1861 Captured and exchanged	18 Jan. 1864	2	5	
	15793.	√COLBERT, Samuel Cockeysville, Balto., Co., Md.	75	78	Private Heart disease	K	13 Md. Inf.	18 Sep. 1861 Was reenlisted Sand Hook 1864	18 Jan. 1864	2	5	
June 6	15794.	AMBROSE, Joshua Cockeysville, Balto., Co., Md.	68	69	Private Rheumatism	D	8 Md. Inf.	30 Aug. 1862	31 May 1865	2	7	1
June 7	15795.	TRACY, William Texas, Baltimore Co., Md.	84	87	Private	B	3 Md. Inf.	23 Mar. 1865 Objection made to reenlistment	28 July 1865		4	5
June 9	15796.	JOHNSON, Bugauerie Cockeysville, Balto., Co., Md.	97	103	Private By this certificate	D	28 U. S. Vol.	20 May 1864 Excluded from all pay on certificate	8 Nov. 1865	1	5	18
	15797.	JOICE, Lewis C. Oregon, Baltimore Co.	112	118	Purnell Legion Private Gun shot wound in left leg	F	Md. Inf.	21 Oct. 1861 Served in Purnell Legion	24 Oct. 1864			

Special Schedule. Surviving Soldiers, Sailors, and Marines, and Widows, etc.

Page

S. D.: ; E. D.: ; Minor Civil Division.:

		1	2	3	4	5	6	7	8	9		
										Yrs	Mos	Dys
June 10	15798.	KURTZ, Thomas Oregon, Balto., Co., Md.	122	128	Private Exposure, knocked down by shell	A	128 Penn. Inf.	5 Aug. 1862 Suffered four shell wounds	19 May 1863		9	14
	15799.	SCHOELKOPF, John Shawan, Balto., Co., Md.	126	133	Private	Bat- talion	Light Art. Md. Vol.	13 Aug. 1862	17 June 1865	2	10	4

Date	No.	Name		House No.	Family No.	Rank	Company	Regiment or Vessel	Enlistment	Discharge	Yrs	Mos	Days
	15800.	Mary R. Ruff, widow of RUFF, John M. Shawan, Balto., Co., Md.	133	141		Private Disability from exposure	B	4 Md. Inf.	25 Aug. 1862	Mar. 1863 He died 1888		7	
	15801.	FAN, Jesse Shawan, Balto., Co., Md.	140	148		Private	H	Inf. 45 U. S. Col. T.	8 Aug. 1864	15 Aug. 1865	1		7
June 11	15802.	DORSEY, George Shawan, Balto., Co., Md.	141	149		Private Ruptured	I	28 Ind. Inf.	28 July 1864	10 Nov. 1865 Discharged at Corpus Christi Texas	1	3	12
June 13	15803.	UHLER, Johnzy Shawan, Balto., Co., Md.	151	160		Private	D	7 Md. Inf.	20 Aug. 1862	31 May 1865	2	9	11
	15804.	Charlotte, widow of CAREY, Edward W. Oregon, Baltimore Co., Md.	175	187		Civilian Cook			186 3 Brigade Sickles Division	186			
	15805.	POWELL, George W. Oregon, Baltimore Co., Md.	176	188		Private Effects of sun stroke in service	D	43 Penn. Inf.	Mar. 1863	1865	1	10	
	15806.	PARKER, Jacob Oregon, Baltimore Co., Md.	178	190		Private Right knee sprained	8	177 Ken. Inf.	17 Mar. 1865	Mar. 1866	1		
June 16	15807.	DONNELLY, Patrick Butler, Baltimore, Co., Md.	181	193		Private		Penn. Inf.	186 Served in Purn Reg. 5 months	186			
	15808.	CHASE, Thomas Cockeysville, Balto., Co., Md.	202	215					186	186			
	15809.	Sarah Timmis, widow of TIMMIS, Henry Cockeysville, Balto., Co., Md.							186 Served 1 yr and was killed	186			
June 18	15810.	MAY, William A. Cockeysville, Balto., Co., Md.	206	219		Private Incipuit - phithsis	A	38 Mass. Inf.	29 July 1861	7 Jan. 1863	1	9	8
June 30	15811.	RESSLER, Peter Butler P. O. Balto., Co., Md.	222	237		Private Typhoid fever			186 Discharged winter 1862	186			

Page No. 1
Supervisor's District No. 1
Enumeration District No. 434

Eleventh Census of the United States

SPECIAL SCHEDULE
SURVIVING SOLDIERS, SAILORS, AND MARINES, AND WIDOWS, ETC

Persons who served in the Army, Navy, and Marine Corps of the United States during the war of the rebellion (who are survivors), and widows of such persons, in   2nd Precinct 8th Dist.   County of   Baltimore   ,
State of   Maryland.   enumerated in June 1890

Geo. C. Duncan
Enumerator

	Name			Rank	Co.	Regiment	Enlisted	Discharged	Yrs	Mos	Dys
15812.	PATTERSON, Henry Texas	5	6 Hand hurt	Blacksmith	C	3 Md. Cav.	unk unk 1863	unk unk 1865	2		
15813.	KELLEY, Thomas F. (Conf) Timonium	24	27 Rheumatism	Private	B	2 Md. Cav.	186	186			
15814.	FISHPAW, William Towson, Md.	64	68	Private	E	2 Md. Inf.	Aug. 21 1862	June 15 1865	2	9	24
15815.	RUHL, Henry Albert Brooks	77	83	Private	E	2 Md. Inf.	Aug 30 1862	June 15 1865	2	10	
15816.	BROOKS, Albert Balto., Co., Alms House	77	83	Private	B	19 Md. Inf.	May 21 1864	Feby 1867	2	9	
15817.	STANTON, Edward Balto., Co., Alms House			Private	B	3 Md. Inf.	1862	1863	1		
15818.	ARCHABALD, James Balto., Co., Alms House			Private			1862	1865	3		
15819.	SHANNON, H. P.			Private	B	8 Md. Inf.	Aug. 1861	Aug. 1863	2		
15820.	GRUBER, Henry Balto., Co., Alms House			Private	G		1864	1865	1		
15821.	SHERHOLT, Henry			Private	F	1 Md. Calv.	Sept. 1861	1863	2		
15822.	HINTON, Daniel Baltimore Co., Alms House			Private	B	9 Md. Inf.	1862	1864	2		
15823.	FORDYCE, J. N. Baltimore Co., Alms House		Rheumatism	Captain	K	1 W. Va. Cav.	Oct. 15 1861	July 8 1865	3	9	

Special Schedule. Surviving Soldiers, Sailors, and Marines, and Widows, etc.

Page 1   S. D.: 1   ; E. D.: 434   ; Minor Civil Division.: 2nd Precinct 8th Dist.

	1	2	3	4	5	6	7	8	9
									Yrs Mos Dys
	15824. SMITH, John Balto., Co., Alms House		None	Private	A	23 Dis. C.	Nov. 1864	1865	1
	15825. DORSEY, John Balto., Co., Alms House			Sailor Private		Ram Atlanta	1864	1865	1
92	15826. *WILLIAMS, George Balto., Co., Alms House		None	U. S. Sol.			186	186	
24	15827. *KELLY, Thomas F. 2nd Precint Baltimore		None	U. S. Sol.			186	186	

3	15828.	*McGLONE, Bernard F. 2nd Precint Baltimore	U. S. Sol. None		186	186	
92	15829.	*DORSEY, John Baltimore Co., Alms House	Sailor		186	186	
92	15830.	*WIGHTING, George Baltimore Co., Alms House	Crippled		186	186	
92	15831.	*KEHOE, John Baltimore Co., Alms House	No. Crippled		186	186	
92	15832.	*SHANNON, Henry P. Baltimore Co., Alms House	U. S. Sol. Rhuematism		186	186	
92	15833.	*NASGO, Charles Baltimore Co., Alms House	Crippled		186	186	
92	15834.	*KANE, James Baltimore Co., Alms House	No Crippled		186	186	
92	15835.	*ARMSTRONG, Solomon Baltimore Co., Alms House	No		186	186	

Page No. 1
Supervisor's District No. 1
Enumeration District No. 435

Eleventh Census of the United States

SPECIAL SCHEDULE
SURVIVING SOLDIERS, SAILORS, AND MARINES, AND WIDOWS, ETC.

Persons who served in the Army, Navy, and Marine Corps of the United States during the war of the rebellion (who are survivors), and widows of such persons, in Lutherville County of Baltimore State of Maryland. enumerated in June 1890

Jas. P. Reese
Enumerator

1	2	3	4	5	6	7	8	9
								Yrs Mos Dys
15836. POWELL, Bennett Lutherville, Md.	Bennett Casten (name of) (his master) real name		Private	A	(U. S.) 10th Va. Vol.	Feb. 2 1864	May 17 1866 Took data from his discharge blank	2 3 15
15837. TALBOTT, J. Fred. C. (Conf) Lutherville, Md.			Private	F	(Conf) 2nd Md. Cav.	July 12 1864	May 15 1865	
15838. TAYLOR, Robt. Franklin Lutherville, Md.			Private	K	29 Ill. Inf. (U.S.)	186	186 Under Capt. Dunn and Lieut. Aikens	1 0 0
15839. CHANEY, Charles Lutherville, Md.	Lost sight of left eye from disease contracted in service - pension pending		Private	K	28 U. S. C. T. Inf.	186	186 Taken from pension card	

	1	2	3	4	5	6	7	8	9		
15840.	TURNER, Jas. H. (Conf) Lutherville, Md.			Lieut.	K	10 Va. Cav.	June	1861	Apr. 11 1865		
15841.	KIDD, George Texas, Balto., Co., Md.			Private	C	6th Penn. Art.	Sep.	1864	June 1865 Under Capt. Evans & Lieut. Baden	10	0
15842.	DAVIS, Patrick Texas, Balto., Co., Md.			Corporal Shot between the ankle and knee	G	1st Mass. Cav.	Nov.	1863	June 1865	1 8	0
15843.	RYAN, Lauty Texas, Balto., Co., Md.			Private Wounded with sabre		9 Mass.	July	1861	1863	2	
15844.	WILCOX, Elias Texas, Balto., Co., Md.			Private Rheumatism & disbites & piles	A9	Volunteers 35 New York	Sept. 20 1861		July 1865 Under Capt. Little	3 10	
15845.	Widow of U. S. (Soldier) WILHELM, Emma Brookenville, Balto., Co., Md.			Wounded at Gettysburg				186	186 Has applied for pension		
15846.	Elizabeth R. Stevenson, wid. STEVENSON, John M. Riders, Balto., Co., Md.			Major Wounded at Gettysburg		Cavalres Infantry 3rd Maryland	May	1861	July 1865	4 2	
15847.	ARMACOST, Melchior Timonisum, Balto., Co., Md.			Private	E	Volunteer 2 E. S. Md.	Aug. 15 1862		June 15 1865	2 10	

Special Schedule. Surviving Soldiers, Sailors, and Marines, and Widows, etc.

Page

S. D.: ; E. D.: ; Minor Civil Division.:

	1	2	3	4	5	6	7	8	9		
										Yrs Mos	Dys
15848.	BAUBLITZ, Cornelius Brooklandwills, Balto., Co.			Private	B	4th Maryland	Aug.	1862	186		6
15849.	ROBINSON, John H. Brooklandwills, Balto., Co.			Private	A	Purnell Legion Cavalry	Dec. 3 1861		Dec. 10 1864	3	
15850.	STEINHAGEN, Richard Brooklandville, Balto., Co.			Purnell Legion Private F Shoulder & right foot crushed		Infantry	Oct. 21 1861		May 15 1863 Under Captain McCallister	2 7	
15851.	*THOMAS, Richard Lutherville, Md.	47	49	Signal Corps U. S. A.		See not on pop sched.		186	186		
15852.	*HALL, Perry Lutherville, Md.	73	77	Sailor U. S.				186	186		
15853.	*JONES, Edward Brooklandville, Md.	178	183					186	186		

	1									
15854.	*NASH, John W.	189	195					186	186	
	Timonium, Md.									
	widow									
15855.	*WEIMEISTER, Anna R.	240	246					186	186	
	Lutherville, Md.									

Page No. 1
Supervisor's District No. 1
Enumeration District No. 436

Eleventh Census of the United States

SPECIAL SCHEDULE
SURVIVING SOLDIERS, SAILORS, AND MARINES, AND WIDOWS, ETC.

Persons who served in the Army, Navy, and Marine Corps of the United States during the war of the rebellion (who are survivors), and widows of such persons, in   1st Prc. 9th Dist.   County of   Baltimore   ,
State of   Maryland.   enumerated in June 1890

J. Fredk. Smith
Enumerator

	1	2	3	4	5	6	7	8	9		
									Yrs	Mos	Dys
15856.	PETTICORD, Joshua	4	4	Private	H	8th Md. Inf.	13 Oct. 1862	27 Aug. 1863		10	14
	Govanstown										
15857.	BULLINGER, William H.	113	116	Private	G	N. Y. 1st Marine Arty	15 Mch 1862	16 Mch 1863	1	00	
	Govanstown	Paralysis of leg & side									
15858.	MANGANO, Lazzara	99	102	Private	B	5th N. Y. Artil	24 Jan. 1862	1 Mch 1865	3	1	7
	Govanstown										
15859.	*DIFFENDERFER, Henry H.	95	98				186	186			
	1st Pre. 9th Div., Md.										
15860.	*KING, William	102	105				186	186			
	1st Pre. 9th Div., Md.										
15861.	*BRAINARD, Edgar J.	113	116				186	186			
	1st Pre. 9th Div., Md.										
15862.	*HARE, Edwan	114	117				186	186			
	1st Pre. 9th Div., Md.										
15863.	*DULTON, George F.	63	66				186	186			
	1st Pre. 9th Div., Md.										
15864.	*MANNING, George O.	61	64				186	186			
	1st Pre. 9th Div., Md.										
15865.	*LEAHY, Rebecca C.	47	50				186	186			
	1st Pre. 9th Div., Md.										

1653

Eleventh Census of the United States

Supervisor's District No. 1
Enumeration District No. 437

SPECIAL SCHEDULE
SURVIVING SOLDIERS, SAILORS, AND MARINES, AND WIDOWS, ETC.

Persons who served in the Army, Navy, and Marine Corps of the United States during the war of the rebellion (who are survivors), and widows of such persons, in Part 3rd Prect. 9th District, County of Baltimore State of Maryland. enumerated in June 1890

William H. Flayhart
Enumerator

	1	2	3	4	5	6	7	8	9 Yrs	Mos	Dys
15866.	PARLETT, William J. Govanstown	77	82 Shot in right cheek	Private	G	1 Md. Inf.	Sept. 1864	May 1865	0	8	
15867.	JAMES, William H. Govanstown	80	86	Private	E & B	11 Md. Inf.	May 1866	June 1865	1	1	
15868.	HENRY, William P. Govanstown	81	87 Hard hearing	Brigade Wagon Master		3rd Brigade 1st Div. 6th Army Corp.	July 1861	1864	3	8	
15869.	DAVIS, Archibald J. Govanstown	114	119	Corp.	D	11 Md. Inf.	May 1863	Sept. 1865	2	3	
15870.	BETZ, John Govanstown	115	120 Feet frosted	Private	B	2 Md. Inf.	Oct. 1862	1865	3	8	
15871.	YASTER, Charles M. Govanstown	123	128 Rupture	Sergeant	A	Cal. 1 Md. P. H. B.	June 1861	June 1865	4		
15872.	VANCE, William T. Govanstown	142	147	Private		3 Md. Inf.	Dec. 1861	June 1865	3	6	
15873.	WILSON, Turner Govanstown	153	158	Private	17 Am C	32 Wis. Inf.	June 1862	June 1865	3		
15874.	WELLS, Henry Govanstown	153	158	Sailor		Massidonia	1862	June 1865	3		
15875.	WATKINS, Daniel R. Govanstown	153	158 Flesh wound left leg	Private	A	4 Mass. Inf.	Sept. 1861	June 1865	3	9	
15876.	GITTINGS, William Govanstown	154	159 Right brest	Private	C	23 D. C. Inf.	1863	1865	2		
15877.	BURRUSS, William J. Govanstown	155	160	Seaman		DeSota	18 Aug. 1865	26 Aug. 1868	3		8

Special Schedule. Surviving Soldiers, Sailors, and Marines, and Widows, etc.

Page

	1	2	3	4	5	6	7	8	9		
									Yrs	Mos	Dys
15878.	RYE, Harry C. Govanstown	159	164 No.	Musician	K	3 Md. Inf.	28 Feb. 1864	29 May 1865	1	3	6

Page No. 1
Supervisor's District No. 1
Enumeration District No. 438

Eleventh Census of the United States

SPECIAL SCHEDULE
SURVIVING SOLDIERS, SAILORS, AND MARINES, AND WIDOWS, ETC.

Persons who served in the Army, Navy, and Marine Corps of the United States during the war of the rebellion (who are survivors), and widows of such persons, in 3rd Prect. 9th Dist. , County of Baltimore , State of Maryland. enumerated in June 1890

Charles L. Shanklin
Enumerator

	1	2	3	4	5	6	7	8	9		
									Yrs	Mos	Dys
15879.	GREEN, John A. Towson, Maryland	11	14	Private	C	10 Md. Inf.	10 Mar. 1863	10 Apr. 1864	1	1	0
15880.	MORRIS, Dapprich Bosley, Balto., Co., Md.	17	20	Corp.	F	1 M. C.	4 Sep. 1861	20 Oct. 1864	3	1	16
15881.	WOOTERS, Daniel Bosley, Balto., Co., Md.	24	27	Private	G	1 M. R.	Oct. 1861	1863	1	6	
15882.	PHIPPS, Alfred Towson, Maryland	25	28	Private	A	9 M. R.	18 Jn. 1863	23 F. 1864		9	
15883.	JONES, David Towson, Maryland	26	29	Private		unable to find	186	186			
15884.	KELSO, George H. Towson, Maryland	27	30	Private		unable to find	186	186			
15885.	KELLIM, Samuel A. Towson, Maryland	28	32	Private	C	7 M. R.	1862	1865	3		
15886.	GURNS, William H. Loch Raven, Maryland	16	20	Serg.	A	1 M. B.	25 Aug. 1861	25 Sep. 1865	4	1	
15887.	LYONS, John R. Loch Raven, Maryland	41	47	Private	A	1 M. R.	1862	1865	3		
15888.	HEDGE, George Loch Raven, Maryland	55	61	'Private Rheumatism contracted suffered ever since discharge	I	3 M. C.	1862	1864	2	6	
15889.	Sarah J., widow of BURKE, Nicholas Towson, Maryland	56	62	Captain	A	1 Gilmor B.	1862	1865	3		

15890.	SLADE, Abraham Towson, Maryland		65	72	Private	I	9 M. V.	6 July 1863	23 F 1864	6		

Special Schedule. Surviving Soldiers, Sailors, and Marines, and Widows, etc.

Page 2   S. D.: 1 ; E. D.: 438 ; Minor Civil Division.:

		1	2	3	4	5	6	7	8	9		
										Yrs	Mos	Dys
15891.	CHENWITH, Thomas J. Towson, Md.		71 Rheumatism	78	Private	B	1 M. R.	5 Dec. 1862	5 Sep. 1863 Suffered ever since discharge		9	
15892.	Lena, widow of BRICKNER, John Towson, Md.		83	91			unable to find	186	186			
15893.	BAYNE, William Towson, Md.		84	92	Sergant	D	7 M. R.	14 Aug. 1862	9 June 1865	2	9	26
15894.	CARTER, Uriah Towson, Md.		85 Rheumatism	93	Corp.	E	2 M. C.	29 June 1863	31 Feb. 1864 Disabled from work		8	
15895.	CARTER, Dennis Loch Raven, Md.		88	96	Private	E	2 M. C.	28 June 1863	31 Feb. 1864		8	
15896.	McCOMSEY, Mathias Carney, Md.		103 Piles	111	Private	H	152 Pen. V.	24 Aug. 1864	12 June 1865 Suffered ever since discharge		9	12
15897.	MILLER, Frederick Carney, Md.		131	146	Private		unable to find	186	186			
15898.	MASSENBURG, Richard C. Towson, Md.		173	189	1 Lieut.	A	Finleys Batt.	31 March 1863	11 May 1865	2	1	11
15899.	REED, William H. W. Towson, Md.		156	171	Private	F	12 V. Reg.	1861	1865	4		
15900.	YOUNG, Charles (colored) Towson, Md.		188	209	Private	B	19 U. S.	2 Nov. 1863	20 Jan. 1866	2	2	17
15901.	HAMMOND, Milbury (colored) Towson, Md.		216	236	Corp.	G	19 U. S.	1 Nov. 1865	186			
15902.	HICKS, Benjamin (colored) Towson, Md.		188	209	Private	C	28 U. S.	1 July 1864	1 Oct. 1865	1	3	0
15903.	HOWARD, Joshua (colored) Towson, Md.		221	241	Private	B	38 unable to read	186	186			
15904.	GOODWIN, John Towson, Md.		222	242	Corporal	A	1 M. V.	28 Feb. 1864	2 July 1865	1	5	2

Special Schedule. Surviving Soldiers, Sailors, and Marines, and Widows, etc.

Page

S. D.: 1   ; E. D.: 438   ; Minor Civil Division.:

	1	2	3	4	5	6	7	8	9
									Yrs Mos Dys
15905.	BROOKS, Albert A. (colored) Towson, Md.	225	245	Private	E	19 U. S.	May 1864	Feb. 1866	
15906.	MACK, Henry (colored) Towson, Md.	226	249	Private	A	9 U. S.	15 Oct. 1864	1 Nov. 1865	11 16
15907.	CHANEY, Louis colored Towson, Md.	227	250				186	186	
15908.	JOHNSON, Anthony colored Towson, Md.	228	252				186	186	
15909.	GREYS, Redmond colored Towson, Md.	234	261				186	186	
15910.	PARKS, John A. Loch Raven, Md.	241	268	Private		unable to find	186	186	
15911.	*WEEKS, William 3 Prect. 9 Dist.	8	9	Sailor			186	186	

Page No. 1
Supervisor's District No. 1
Enumeration District No. 439

Eleventh Census of the United States

SPECIAL SCHEDULE
SURVIVING SOLDIERS, SAILORS, AND MARINES, AND WIDOWS, ETC

Persons who served in the Army, Navy, and Marine Corps of the United States during the war of the rebellion (who are survivors), and widows of such persons, in   3rd Precinct. 9th Dist.   , County of   Balto.   ,
State of   Maryland.   enumerated in June 1890

Geo. H. Horne
Enumerator

	1	2	3	4	5	6	7	8	9
									Yrs Mos Dys
15912.	BURNINE, James 33 Jackson St. Balto., City	2	2	Private	F	14 Ten. Inf.	(5) May 1861	end of war 1865	
15913.	SMITH, Amos Columbia, Howard Co., Md.	2	2	Private	L	11 R. I. Art.	1 1 1863	end of war 1865 Contracted chills & fever	1 1
15914.	TOMPHSON, Josiah # 16 Church St. Balto., City	2	2	Private Shot in privates	A	7 Md. Inf.	1 1 1862	end of war 1865 Was sent to jail as insane but Doctor examined him & pronounced him sane	3 4
15915.	LINZEY, James H. Towson, Balto., Co., Md.	6	6	Private	C	1 Md. Inf.	June 1863	4 5 1865	1 11

15916.	HINES, Francis M Towson, Balto., Co.,	29	29	Corporal Shot in left foot & right hand	D	7 Md. Inf		15 Aug. 1862	31 May 1865	2	9	16
15917.	WARD, Felix Towson, Balto., Co.,	31	31	Sailor Chronic diarrhoea		U. S. Lancaster		unknown 186	unknown 186 Enlistment discharge & service papers are at Washington	unknown		
15918.	McINTOSH, David G. (Conf) Towson, Balto., Co.,	41	41	Col.		1st S. Car. Inf.	1	3 1861	unknown 186 Does not remember date of transfere	end of war		
15919.	√ McINTOSH, David G. (Conf) Towson, Balto., Co.,	41	41	Col.		2 & 3 Corp. Army of Virg.		unknown 186	disbanded 186	end of war		
15920.	YELLOTT, John I. Towson, Balto., Co.	44	44	Major Shot on left arm		Inf. 1 Md. P. H. B.	9	1861	10 1864 Surgeon's certificate discharge for rheumatism	3	1	
15921.	GRANT, George W. Towson, Balto., Co.	60	60	Private	D	unk Indiana Inf.		unk unk 1864	unk unk 1865	1	unk	unk
15922.	PERRIE, Albert W. Towson, Balto., Co.	72	72	Private Slight wound in chin		1 Mas. Art.	7	1861	Oct. 1864	3	2	
15923.	WHITTLE, Samuel N. Towson, Balto., Co.	75	75	1st Lieut. Shot in left shoulder		7 Md. Inf.		10 14 1862	5 31 1865	2	9	17

Special Schedule. Surviving Soldiers, Sailors, and Marines, and Widows, etc.

Page

2   S. D.:   ; E. D.:   ; Minor Civil Division.:

	1	2	3	4	5	6	7	8	9		
									Yrs	Mos	Dys
15924.	SEIPP, George W. Towson Balto., Co., Md.	82	82	Sergt. Shot in left fore arm	G	7 Md. Inf.	5 27 1861	9 24 1864 Arm has been amputated	3	3	29
15925.	Margaret A. Dunning DUNNING, John Towson Balto., Co., Md.	88	88	Private	D	7 Md. Inf.	8 21 1862	unk unk 1865	3	unk	unk
15926.	BROWN, Ezra F. Towson Balto., Co., Md.	91	91	Private	G	2 Md. Inf.	8 9 1861	8 8 1864 Suffering from fistula resulting from chronic diarrhoea contracted in war	3		
15927.	DUNPHY, Richard G. Towson Balto., Co., Md.	92	92	2nd Lieut.	D	7 Md.Inf.	8 14 186	6 unk 1865 Chronic rheumatism contracted in war	2	10	
15928.	PRATT, Joseph Towson Balto., Co., Md.	100	100	Private	A	Col 1 Miss. Inf.	unk 1862	unk 1865 Discharge papers lost	2	unk	
15929.	TIMMONS, Charles T. Towson Balto., Co., Md.	109	109	Private	A	Col 39 Md. Inf.	Mch unk 1864	Dec. unk 1865 Chronic diarrhoea contracted in war	1	9	unk

#	1	2	3	4	5	6	7	8	9 Yrs Mos Dys
15930.	ROBINSON, Adam F. Towson Balto., Co., Md.	110	110 None	Private	C	Col 39 Md. Inf.	April unk 1864	July unk 1865	1 3 unk
15931.	BESS, Benjamin Towson Balto., Co., Md.	118	118	Private	E	Col 30 Md. Inf.	unk 1864	unk 1865 Discharge papers lost	unk
15932.	CARVALL, Charles Towson Balto., Co., Md.	123	123 None	Corp.	H	Col 39 Md. Inf.	3 unk 1863	Dec unk 1865 Discharge papers lost	2 9 unk
15933.	Caleb Bailey in war BIRD, Caleb comes as names Towson Balto., Co., Md.	128	128 None	Private	unk	unknown	unk unk 186	unk unk 186 Papers lost	1 6 unk
15934.	TAYLOR, Samuel Towson Balto., Co., Md.	131	131 None	Private	G	Col. 39 U. S. Inf.	1 20 1865	11 6 1865	0 9 17
15935.	BROWN, David Towson Balto., Co., Md.	115	115	Landsman Cut in leg and side		Peguoit	9 unk 1862	9 unk 1865	1 0 unk
15936.	TOMAY, Sylvester C. Towson Balto., Co., Md.	87	87 None	Private	E	1 Md. (Conf) Inf.	5 21 186	5 unk 1865	4 0 0
15937.	BEDFORD, William D. Towson Balto., Co., Md.	140	140 None	Private		Coles Cavalry	unk unk 1862	unk unk 1865	3 unk unk

Special Schedule. Surviving Soldiers, Sailors, and Marines, and Widows, etc.

Page

S. D.:   ; E. D.:   ; Minor Civil Division.:

#	1	2	3	4	5	6	7	8	9 Yrs Mos Dys
15938.	O'KEEFE, Matthew (Conf) Towson Balto., Co., Md.	142	142 None	Chaplain		Mahone Brigade	unk 1861	unk unk 1865	4 unk
15939.	FLANNIGAN, Patrick F. (Conf) Towson Balto., Co., Md.	132	132 None	Private		1 S. Car. L. A.	unk 1861	unk unk 1865	4 unk
15940.	JARRETT, Dr. James H. Towson Balto., Co., Md.	89	89	Surgeon Injury to abdomen, resulting in rupture		7 Md. Inf.	Oct. unk 1861	April unk 1864	2 6 unk
15941.	Hester A. Johnson JOHNSON, Frank Towson Balto., Co., Md.	147	147	Private Husband killed in war	G	39 U. S. Col.	unk 186	unk unk 186	unk
15942.	BURTON, John Towson Balto., Co., Md.	151	151 None	Private	E	2 Md. Cav.	7 7 1863	1 31 1864	0 6 24
15943.	SWENE, Amon Towson Balto., Co., Md.	157	157 None	Private	A	Purnell Legion	11 20 1861	7 26 1865	4 8 6
15944.	DANSBURY, Thomas Towson Balto., Co., Md.	165	165 None	Cook		Mackinaro	unk 186	3 31 1865	unk

No.	Name / Address	Col2	Col3	Rank	Co.	Regiment	Enlisted	Discharged	Yrs	Mos	Dys
15945.	LEWIS, John W. — Towson Balto., Co., Md.	167	167	Private	E	5 Md. Ins.	unk 1863	unk unk 1865	unk		
	None										
15946.	GLADMON, John W. — Towson Balto., Co., Md.	173	173	Private	L	Md. Cav.	9 30 1862	8 8 1865	2	10	22
	None										
15947.	√GLADMON, John W. — Towson Balto., Co., Md.	173	173	Private		Dist. Union Rifles	4 16 1861	7 unk 1861	0	3	unk
15948.	LEWIS, Jesse — Towson Balto., Co., Md.	175	175	Private	E	5 Md. Inf.	9 unk 1861	9 unk 1864	3	0	unk
	Shot in right fore arm										
15949.	DOXZEN, Daniel M. — Riders Balto., Co., Md.	183	183	Private	I	1 Md. Inf.	11 2 1861	11 2 1864	3	0	0
	Shot 3 times in war										
15950.	SHEETS, Jacob — Riders Balto., Co., Md.	205	205	Private		3rd Penna. Battery	1 unk 1862	6 25 1865	3	6	unk
	None										
15951.	MEADES, James — Riders Balto., Co., Md.			Private	H	30 Md. Col. Vol.	3 10 1864	7 unk 1865	1	4	unk
	None						Chronic rheumatism contract in war				

Special Schedule. Surviving Soldiers, Sailors, and Marines, and Widows, etc.

Page 3   S. D.: ; E. D.: ; Minor Civil Division.:

1	2	3	4	5	6	7	8	9
								Yrs Mos Dys
15952. HERMAN, Emanuel — Towson Balto., Co., Md.	210	210	Private	C	3. 18 (U.S.) Inf.	10 28 1861	10 28 1864	3
Slight wound in neck (shot)								
15953. √HERMAN, Emanuel — Towson Balto., Co., Md.	210	210	Captain	??	103 Penna. Inf.	11 unk 1864	9 unk 1865	0 10 unk
15954. MURRAY, Thomas — Towson Balto., Co., Md.			Private	C	13 Md. Inf.	1 unk 1865	6 unk 1865	0 6 unk
None								
15955. WIEGER, William — 813 E. Balto., St. Balto., City	289	289	Musican		2 Mich. Inf.	7 unk 1861	8 unk 1862	1 1 unk
							Drawing pension for heart trouble	
15956. √WIEGER, William — 813 E. Balto., St. Balto., City	289	289	Musican		2 U.S.A.	10 26 1863	10 26 1868	5 0 0
15957. KAPP, Hosea — Union Station Balto., City	302	302	Musician		5 Penna.	8 unk 1861	7 1862	11
None								
15958. *FOOT, William — Lutherville Balto., Co., Md.	156	156	Private			186	186	
15959. *MATHEWS, Benjamin — Towson Balto., Co., Md.	129	129	Private			186	186	
15960. *BROWN, Aaron — 3rd Prct. 9 Dist. Balto., Co., Md.	255	255	Private			186	186	

Note:-The provision of the act of March 1, 1889, under which this special enumeration of survivors of the war of the rebelloin is made, reads as follows:

That said Superintendent shall under the authority of the Secretary of the Interior, cause to be taken on a special schedule of inquiry, according to such form as he may prescribe, the names, organizations, and length of service of those who had served in the Army, Navy, or Marines Corps of the United States in the war of the rebellion, and who are survivors at the time of said inquiry, and the widows of soldiers, sailors, or marines.

The entries concerning each survivor or widow should be carefully and accurately made, so that the printed reports may contain only thoroughly trustworthy information.

Spaces are provided on this special schedule for the entry of fifty names, or more properly, term of service. The spaces are numbered consecutively from 1 to 50, and cover the four pages comprised in each schedule. The inquiries made concerning each survivor or widow call for the repetition of the number of the house and family as returned on the general population schedule (No. 1), the name, rank company, regiment or vessel, date of enlistment, date of discharge, and length of service (in years, months, and days) on the upper half of each page, and the post-office address, disability incurred, and general remarks on the lower half of each page. The column headed "Remarks" is intended to be used to cover any points not included in the forgoing inquires, and which are necessary to a complete statement of a person's term of service in any one organization.

In the case of persons having served in more than one organization, use as many spaces as may be necessary to cover their various terms of service. In the case of widows of deceased soldiers, sailors, or marines, make the entry of her name on the dotted lines, as follows: Mary J., widow of filling out the record of his service during the war, and giving under "post-office address" the Present address of his widow. BROWN, James H.

Page No. 1
Supervisor's District No. 1
Enumeration District No. 440

Eleventh Census of the United States

SPECIAL SCHEDULE
SURVIVING SOLDIERS, SAILORS, AND MARINES, AND WIDOWS, ETC

Persons who served in the Army, Navy, and Marine Corps of the United States during the war of the rebellion (who are survivors), and widows of such persons, in Election District 9 , County of Baltimore
State of Maryland. enumerated in June 1890

Geo. W. Hook
Enumerator

	1	2	3	4	5	6	7	8	9 Yrs	Mos	Dys
15961.	BELL, William Rider Balto., Co., Md.	7	7	Private Wounded in right shoulder	F	Purnell Legion	24 Oct. 1861	29 Oct. 1864	3	0	5
15962.	SMITH, James Brooklandville Balto., Co., Md.	24	24	Private	H	8 Md. Inf.	10 Nov. 1862	27 Aug. 1863	0	9	17
15963.	BUTLER, James Rider Balto., Co., Md.	32	32	Private	F	38 Md. Inf.	15 Dec. 1864	15 Sept. 1865	0	9	0
15964.	RODGERS, Edward N. Lake Roland Balto., Co., Md.	49	49				186	186			
15965.	AKEHURST, Charles Mt. Washington Balto., Co., Md.	57	57	Private	I	8 Md. Inf.	29 Oct. 1862	8 Aug. 1863	0	9	21
15966.	DOTSON, Thomas Lake Roland Balto., Co., Md.	72	72	Wounded in breast			186	186 Pension agent has papers			
15967.	REED, Oliver C. Lake Roland Balto., Co., Md.	86	86	Private			April 1865	June 1865			

Page No. 1
Supervisor's District No. 1
Enumeration District No. 441

Eleventh Census of the United States

SPECIAL SCHEDULE
SURVIVING SOLDIERS, SAILORS, AND MARINES, AND WIDOWS, ETC.

Persons who served in the Army, Navy, and Marine Corps of the United States during the war of the rebellion (who are survivors), and

widows of such persons, in   Election District   , County of   Baltimore.
State of   Maryland.   enumerated in June 1890

Geo. W. Hook
Enumerator

	1	2	3	4	5	6	7	8	9			
										Yrs	Mos	Dys
15968.	WARD, Thomas Waverly	2	2	Private Shot in the head	I	19 U. S. Inf.	June 1863	June 1865 Date of enlistment unknown				
15969.	DIETZ, Christopher 502 Fifth St. Balto., City	5	5	Private	A	6th Md. Inf.	11 Aug. 1862	26 June 1865 Now crippled rheumatism				
15970.	PACE, Pleasant W. (Conf) Mt. Washington Balto., Co., Md.	82	82	Private Shot in right arm	C	14 Va. Inf.	June 1861	Mch 1865 Date of enlistment unknown				
15971.	JOHNSON, William J. Mt. Washington Balto., Co., Md.	86	86	Sargent		Patapsco Md. Inf.	Oct. 1861	Nov. 1864 Date of enlistment unknown				
15972.	APPLEBY, Raisin Mt. Washington Balto., Co., Md.	86	86	Private Rhumatism	F	1 Md. Inf.	27 May 1861	19 May 1864		2	11	23
15973.	PAYNE, Henry O. Mt. Washington Balto., Co., Md.	90	90	Private Kicked horse right side		Artilery 6 Md. Vol.	6 July 1863	19 Jan. 1864			6	13
15974.	HUDSON, Henry Mt. Washington Balto., Co., Md.	88	88	Private	G	10 Md. Vol.	23 June 1863	29 Jan. 1864			7	6
15975.	WOLFENDEN, Thomas Mt. Washington Balto., Co., Md.	94	94	Private	C	8 Md. Inf.	18 Aug. 1862	31 May 1865		2	9	13
15976.	WILLIAMS, George W. Mt. Washington Balto., Co., Md.	98	98	Private	D	4 U. S. Vol.	Oct. 1864	June 1866 Date of enlistment unknown				
15977.	Mary F., widow of BAUGHMAN, Joshua Mt. Washington Balto., Co., Md.	64	64	Private Paralisis	C	1 Md. Inf.	12 June 1861	23 May 1864		2	11	19
15978.	Susan R., widow of HILTABRIDLE, Joseph Mt. Washington Balto., Co., Md.	103	103	Private		unk Inf.	1861	1865 Date of enlistment unknown				
15979.	(Conf) SCHELLING, George B. Mt. Washington Balto., Co., Md.	109	109	Corporal Shot in left thigh	K	23 Va. Inf.	1861	1863 Date of enlistment unknown				

Special Schedule. Surviving Soldiers, Sailors, and Marines, and Widows, etc.

Page

S. D.:   ; E. D.:   ; Minor Civil Division.:

1	2	3	4	5	6	7	8	9

Yrs Mos Dys

No.	Name			Rank	Co.	Regiment	Enlisted	Discharged	Yrs	Mos	Dys
15980.	FRENCH, Oliver Mt. Wshington Balto., Co., Md.	115	115	Private		1 Md. Cavl.	1861	1863 Date of enlistment unknown			
15981.	McSHERRY, Richard M. (Conf) Mt. Washington Balto., Co., Md.	117	117	Private		Va.	186	186 (In) Europe could gain no information			
15982.	FRACTION, Othello Melvale Balto., Co., Md.	148	148	Private	H	40 U. S. Inf.	April 1864	June 1865 Papers in Washington			
15983.	LOUIS, William Melvale Balto., Co., Md.	164	164	Private	C	39 U. S. Inf.	24 Mch. 1864	14 April 1864 Served about 2 years in Navy			21
15984.	HUMPHREYS, Ralph Melvale Balto., Co., Md.	186	186	Private		Md. Inf.	186	186 Papers all lost			
15985.	DALLHON, Lewis Melvale Balto., Co., Md.	183	183	Private		N. Y. Col.	186	1865 Papers stolen			
15986.	CONEY, William Hamden Balto., Co., Md.	197	197	Private	A	10 Md. Inf.	1864	1865 Date of enlistment unknown			
15987.	CASSELL, Alexander Embla Balto., Co., Md.	192	192 Wounded in thigh	Private		4 U. S. Inf.	186	1865 Date of enlistment unknown			
15988.	WHITTINGTON, Joseph Embla Balto., Co., Md.	192	192	Private		4 U. S. Inf.	186	1865 Date of enlistment unknown			
15989.	CARTER, John W. Embla Balto., Co., Md.	196	196	Private		Md. Inf.	186	1865 Papers all lost			
15990.	ALLEN, Christopher Embla Balto., Co., Md.	196	196 Ribs broken	Private		1 Md. Cal.	April 1861	1865 Date of enlistment unknown			
15991.	DAVIS, George N. Embla Balto., Co., Md.	204	204 Back hurt	Private	G	5 Md. Inf.	10 Jan. 1862	5 Feb. 1864	2		25
15992.	LITZINGER, Richard Hamden Balto., Co., Md.	216	216	Private		2 Md. Cal.	186	186 Date of enlistment unknown			
15993.	GETTY, Andrew Melville Balto., Co., Md.	219	219 Wound right arm	Private	F	5 Md. Inf.	Oct. 1861	1865 Date of enlistment unknown			

Special Schedule. Surviving Soldiers, Sailors, and Marines, and Widows, etc.

Page

S. D.: ; E. D.: ; Minor Civil Division.:

	1	2	3	4	5	6	7	8	9		
									Yrs	Mos	Dys
15994.	NACE, Ferdinand Hamden Balto., Co., Md.	218	218	Private Rhumatism	G	1 Md. Vet.	18 Aug. 1862	3 June 1865	2	10	15
15995.	WHITE, William Hamden Balto., Co., Md.	217	217	Private Rhumatism	C	10 Md. Vol.	24 June 1863	29 Jan. 1864		7	5
15996.	BLUCHER, Albert Hamden Balto., Co., Md.	221	221	Private Shot in thigh	F	5 Md. Vol.	18 Jan. 1862	18 Jan. 1865	3		

	1	2	3	4	5	6	7	8	9		
15997.	WILLIAMS, James E. Nohedame Balto., Co., Md.	124	124	Private	K	7 U. S. Inf.	12 Sept. 1863	6 Mch 1865	1	6	6
15998.	CROCKER, Samuel G. 314 North St. Balto., Md.	226	226	Private	G	11 Md. Inf.	30 May 1864	27 Sept. 1864		3	27

Page No.   1
Supervisor's District No. 1
Enumeration District No. 442

Eleventh Census of the United States

SPECIAL SCHEDULE
SURVIVING SOLDIERS, SAILORS, AND MARINES, AND WIDOWS, ETC

Persons who served in the Army, Navy, and Marine Corps of the United States during the war of the rebellion (who are survivors), and widows of such persons, in   1st Precinct 10th District , County of   Baltimore.
State of   Maryland.   enumerated in June 1890

Frank E. Sparks
Enumerator

	1	2	3	4	5	6	7	8	9 Yrs	Mos	Dys
15999.	Mary E. Winstanley, widow of William Winstanley alias PRESTON, Alfred Monkton Balto., Co., Md.	4	4	Fireman		Meantnomah	Dec. 1 1864	Oct. 2 1867	2	10	1
16000.	HOLLENSHADE, Thomas Monkton Balto., Co., Md	18	18	Private	F	Inf. Purnell Legion	Sept. 5 1861	Oct. 24 1864	3	0	19
16001.	HOLLINS, Richard Corbett Balto., Co., Md.	29	31	Private	D	39 Md. Col. Inf.	186	186	1		
16002.	Lucy L. Meek, widow of MEEK, Thomas Corbett Balto., Co., Md.	30	32	Artificer	C	Vol. 50 N. Y. Engin	Dec. 20 1863	Jan. 13 1865	1	5	24
16003.	Lucy L. Meek, widow of √MEEK, Thomas Corbett Balto., Co., Md.	30	32	Artificer	C	Vol. 50 N. Y. Engin	Aug. 25 1861	Dec. 25 1863	2	3	27
16004.	CROSS, Michael Monkton Balto., Co., Md.	36	38	Private	K	5 Md. Inf.	186	186	2		
16005.	Nancy, widow of McCOMAS, John M. White Hall Balto., Co., Md.	56	60	Captain Erysipelas contracted in prison	1	9 Md. Inf.	1863	1864	1	6	
16006.	McMAN, John White Hall Balto., Co., Md.	56	60	Private	G	3 Md. Inf.	Oct. 15 1862	Aug. 3 1863	0	9	19
16007.	√McMAN, John White Hall Balto., Co., Md.	56	60	Private	G	3 Md. Inf.	Apr. 11 1865	May 29 1865	0	1	19
16008.	GIBBS, William H. Phoenix Balto., Co., Md.	88	93	Private Shot through the knee Scurvey contracted from exposure	D	39 Md. Col. Inf.	186	186	1		

	1	2	3	4	5	6	7	8	9		
16009.	TURNBAUGH, John Phoenix Balto. Co., Md.	92	97	Private	I	11 Md. Inf.	Feb. 14 1864	Jan. 15 1865	0	11	1
16010.	Martha J. Vance, widow of VANCE, James Monkton Balto., Co., Md.	114	120	Corporal	G	1 Md. Vol. Inf.	Aug. 12 1862	Jan. 3 1865	2	9	22

Special Schedule. Surviving Soldiers, Sailors, and Marines, and Widows, etc.

Page 2   S. D.: 1 ; E. D.: 442   ; Minor Civil Division.: 1st Precinct 10th District

	1	2	3	4	5	6	7	8	9		
									Yrs	Mos	Dys
16011.	YOUNG, Thomas H. Monkton Balto., Co., Md.	126	132	Private	I	39 Md. Col. Inf.		186	186	1	3	
16012.	O'KEEFE, Thomas Manor Balto., Co., Md.	196	206	Private Asthma contracted from exposure	I	8th Md. Inf.		1861	1862	0	9	0
16013.	WOLFE, John W. Manor Balto., Co., Md.	203	213	Drummer	F	10 Md. Inf.	Aug. 1862	Jan. 1863	0	5	0
16014.	*YOUNG, John T. 10th District	126	136	Private				186	186			

Page No. 1
Supervisor's District No. 1
Enumeration District No. 443

Eleventh Census of the United States

SPECIAL SCHEDULE
SURVIVING SOLDIERS, SAILORS, AND MARINES, AND WIDOWS, ETC.

Persons who served in the Army, Navy, and Marine Corps of the United States during the war of the rebellion (who are survivors), and widows of such persons, in District No. 10 , County of Baltimore,
State of Maryland, enumerated in June 1890

William H. Curtis
Enumerator

	1	2	3	4	5	6	7	8	9		
									Yrs	Mos	Dys
16015.	KONE, William H. Phoenix Balto., Co.			Sergent Gun shot wound	G	F. Md	May 27 1861	Oct. 26 1864 This wound in shoulder & Jan.	3	5	26
16016.	HAWKINS, James Phoenix Balto., Co.			Private	A	87 R. Pa.	Aug. 24 1861	Oct. 13 1864	3		
16017.	AKEHURST, David Phoenix Balto., Co.			Private	G	1 R. M. V.	1861	Sep. 23 1863	2		
16018.	EDWARDS, John Sunny Brook Balto., Co			Private	G	4 R. M. I.	Aug. 11 1863	May 4 1866	2	8	23

No.	Name / Place	Notes	Rank	Co.	Regiment	Enlisted	Discharged	Yrs	Mos	Dys
16019.	BARRY, William / Phoenix		Sergeant	F	1st R. Md.	Sep. 23 1861	Dec. 21 1863 Re-enlisted veteran	2	2	28
16020.	√BARRY, William / Phoenix		Sergeant	F	1st R. Md.	Dec. 24 1863	Aug. 8 1865	1	7	14
16021.	FORD, Francis / Phoenix		Private	G	1st R. M.	Sept. 11 1861	Oct. 4 1864	3	0	23
16022.	WINDER, Hicks / Sunny Brook	Contracted rheumatism	Private	M	27 U. S. Inf.	1863	1865 Lost his discharge papers	2	0	0
16023.	MURRAY, Lewis / Sunny Brook	Contracted rheumatism	Private	G	1st M. Inf.	Feb. 27 1864	July 7 1865 Near 3 month hospital	1	5	20
16024.	WILSON, Gittings / Sweet Air	Contracted rhumatism	Sergeant	G	1 M. Inf.	Aug. 8 1861	July 11 1865 Prisoner at Libby & Bell Island	4	11	3
16025.	JOHNSON, Samuel / Sweet Air		Private	G	4 M. Inf.	Aug. 11 1863	July 11 1865 Lost discharge papers	2	1	0
16026.	ALBAUGH, Charles / Sunny Brook	Contracted rheumatism	Private	B	1 M. Inf.	Oct. 7 1861	July 15 1865	3	9	8

Special Schedule. Surviving Soldiers, Sailors, and Marines, and Widows, etc.

Page

S. D.: ; E. D.: ; Minor Civil Division.:

1	2	3	4	5	6	7	8	9 (Yrs Mos Dys)
16027. KLINE, Joseph / Jacksonville			Contracted rheumatism / Private	I	11 Md. Inf.	July 1 1864	Oct. 1 1864 Enlisted under name Charles Gross	3
16028. TRAPP, John A. / Dulaney Valley			Contracted diarra / Private	M	8 M. Inf.	Oct. 28 1862	Aug. 27 1863	9 29
16029. ECKHART, William / Sunny Brook			Contracted rheumatism / Corporal	K	8 M. Vol.	Oct. 27 1862	Aug. 3 1863	9
16030. BRADRY, Nathan / Sunny Brook			Private	C	7 M. Inf.	Feb. 25 1864	July 7 1865	1 3 12
16031. *URASLETTA, John / Baltimore	248	248				186	186	
16032. *TRACEY, Elijah F. / Baltimore	205	205				186	186	
16033. *NEHIER, John / Baltimore	202	202				186	186	
16034. *AYERS, Henry / Baltimore	169	196				186	186	
16035. *SCERER, John E. / Baltimore	149	149				186	186	

	1	2	3	4	5	6	7	8	9		
16036.	*HANEY, Amos Baltimore	77	77					186	186		

Page No. 1
Supervisor's District No. 1
Enumeration District No. 444

Eleventh Census of the United States

SPECIAL SCHEDULE
SURVIVING SOLDIERS, SAILORS, AND MARINES, AND WIDOWS, ETC

Persons who served in the Army, Navy, and Marine Corps of the United States during the war of the rebellion (who are survivors), and widows of such persons, in 1st Prec. 11 District , County of Baltimore. ,
State of Maryland. enumerated in June 1890

W. O. B. Wright
Enumerator

	1	2	3	4	5	6	7	8	9 Yrs	Mos	Dys
16037.	HALL, John Reckord, Md.	20	21 Rupture	Corporal	G	76 Pena. Vol.	Feb. 1 1861	July 18 1865	4	5	17
16038.	TEMPLE, Benjamin F. Kingsville, Md.	54	52 Rheumatism	Cor.		7 Ma. Vol,	Oct. 25 186	186 Could not get dates of enl. & disc.			
16039.	CLOMAN, James F. Kingsville, Md.	51	54	Private	G	2 Md. Vol.	Oct. 28 1861	186	9		
16040.	GIBSON, Andrew Fork Baltimore Co., Md.	79	83	Private	L	5 U. S. Art.	Apr. 9 1862	July 2 1866	3	9	23
16041.	PREGAL, Mathew Fork Baltimore Co., Md.	151	155	Private	D	3rd Ma. Vol. Bat.	21 Mch 1865	July 31 1865		4	10
16042.	MORRING, Charles Robert Baldwin Balto., Co., Md.	155	159	Corp.	B	3rd Md. P. H. B.	Feb. 24 1862	May 29 1865	3	3	
	Eliza A. Morring, formerly widow of			Sergent	A						
16043.	JOHNSON, William H. Baldwin Balto., Co., Md.	155	159	Private	I	2nd Md. Vol.	Dec. 20 1861	Dec. 20 1865	2		
16044.	BARTEN, Isaac I. Greenwood Balto., Co., Md.	184	188 Rheumatism & failure of sight	Corporal	I	2nd Md. Vol.	Nov. 1 1863	1865 Could not get Mo. & date disc.	2		
16045.	RAYNER, John Greenwood, Md.	206	210			Purnell Md. Eighth Vol.	186	186 Could not get rank, dis. &c.			
16046.	COUNCIL, Jacob D. Summerfield, Md.	216	220 Deafness by artillery	Private	A	Vol. Md. Purnel Light	1864	186 Drafted in 1864, service 11 mos. has lost papers	11		
16047.	SHAFFER, Francis Summerfield, Md.	227	232 Rupture	Private	E	(Corps. Vol.) 20 Vet. Res.	Feb. 6 1862	Feb. 6 1865	3		
16048.	LOWRIE, Alexander W. Fork Baltimore Co., Md.	235	240 Rheumatism	Private	K	28 N. Y. Vol.	May 22 1861	Jne 2 1863	2		11

Special Schedule. Surviving Soldiers, Sailors, and Marines, and Widows, etc.

Page

S. D.: ; E. D.: ; Minor Civil Division.:

	1	2	3	4	5	6	7	8	9
									Yrs Mos Dys
16049.	*BELL, Phillip	168	172	Sol.			186	186	

Page No.
Supervisor's District No. First
Enumeration District No. 445

Eleventh Census of the United States

SPECIAL SCHEDULE
SURVIVING SOLDIERS, SAILORS, AND MARINES, AND WIDOWS, ETC.

Persons who served in the Army, Navy, and Marine Corps of the United States during the war of the rebellion (who are survivors), and widows of such persons, in   11 Dist.   , County of   Baltimore.
State of   Maryland,   enumerated in June 1890

H. Z. Mast
Enumerator

	1	2	3	4	5	6	7	8	9
									Yrs Mos Dys
16050.	GREENBURY, Pearce Glen Arm, Md.	3	3	Private	A	7 Md. Art.	4 Feb. 1862	2 Feb. 1864	
16051.	LEMMEN, George Long Green, Md.	11	11	Private	F	191 Pa. Inf.	Sep. 1862	June 1866	
16052.	MERRYMEN, John W. Gittings, Md.	13	13	Corp.	G	1 Md. Vol.	June 1862	25 June 1866	
16053.	SMALTZER, Martin Long Green, Md.	51	51	Private	F	2 Md. Inf.	July 1861	Aug. 1865	
16054.	BOWERS, Barnhard Long Green, Md.	57	57	Private	E	15 U. S. Inf.	25 Feb. 1864	25 Feb. 1867	
16055.	WOODS, Joseph E. Knoebel, Md.	95	97	Private	E	7 Md. Inf.	31 Aug. 1862	16 Dec. 1862	
16056.	MORROW, John Hydes, Md.	109	112	Private			186	186	
16057.	Isebella Morrow, widow of OWINGS, Joseph (U.S.) Nav Hydes, Md.	109	112				186	186	
16058.	FOARD, Thomas Hydes, Md.	118	121	Private	B	3 Md. Inf.	19 Mar. 1865	15 June 1865	

No.	Name & P.O.	1	2	3	4	5	6	7	8	9
16059.	STREUBEL, Frank Gruinn, Md.	137	140	Corp.	F		1 Md. Calc.	26 Feb. 1864	8 Aug. 1865	
16060.	GORSUCH, William Long Green, Md.	166	169	Private	C		1 Md. Inf.	Nov. 1864	3 July 1865	
16061.	SMITH, Albert Dulaney Valley, Md.				D		39 Md. Inf.	186	186	

Special Schedule. Surviving Soldiers, Sailors, and Marines, and Widows, etc.

Page

S. D.: ; E. D.: ; Minor Civil Division.:

		1	2	3	4	5	6	7	8	9
										Yrs Mos Dys
16062.	DOYLE, Hugh Dulaney Valley P. O., Md.	187	190				17 Md. Art.	2 Aug. 1862	22 Mar. 1863	
16063.	VOFEN, John Fork, Md.	199	202	Private	C		7 Md. Inf.	1862	Aug. 1865	
16064.	HARRIS, Henry C. Long Green, Md.	55	55	Private	G		5 Md. Vol. Inf.	14 Oct. 1861	31 Dec. 1863	
16065.	Reinlisted √HARRIS, Henry C. Long Green, Md.	55	55	Private	G		5 Md.	1 Jan. 1864	1 Sep. 1865	
16066.	*ALLEN, Solomon C. 11 Dist., Md.	129	129					186	186	
16067.	*WEYHOMSER, Gerhart 11 Dist., Md.	98	100					186	186	
16068.	*JOHNSON, John A. 11 Dist., Md.	28	28					186	186	

Page No.
Supervisor's District No. 1
Enumeration District No. 446

Eleventh Census of the United States

SPECIAL SCHEDULE
SURVIVING SOLDIERS, SAILORS, AND MARINES, AND WIDOWS, ETC.

Persons who served in the Army, Navy, and Marine Corps of the United States during the war of the rebellion (who are survivors), and widows of such persons, in   D. 11 - 2nd Precinct   , County of   Baltimore.   ,
State of   Maryland.   enumerated in June 1890

Hy. A. Bachtel
Enumerator

1	2	3	4	5	6	7	8	9
								Yrs Mos Dys

No.	Name & P.O.	2	3	Rank	Co.	Regiment	Enlisted	Discharged	Yrs	Mos
16069.	BOND, Geo. W. Cub Hill, Md.	52	54 Pralysis	Private	K	7th Md. Inf	about March 1863	Oct. 1865 Discharge mislaid	2	6
16070.	BENTON, Francis Cub Hill, Md.	50	50 Shot through rgt lung	Private	G	Md. Vols. Purnell Legion	12 Oct. 1861	12 Nov. 1864	3	
16071.	FOX, George Perry Hall, Md.	15	16 Lost right eye	Corporal	A	1st Md. Inf.	Sept. 1864	3 July 1865		10
16072.	CARROLL, Charles Cub Hill, Md.	51	53 Crippled in both legs	Private		Home Brigade 3rd Md. Potomac	186	186 Papers mislaid		
16073.	MAGLIDT, Henry Cub Hill, Md.	91	93 Chronic rheumatism			Home Brigade 3rd Md. Potomac	March 1862	Mar. 1864 Pension applied for	2	
16074.	WINKLER, Adam Necker, Md.	193	195 Lost right arm, gun shot wound, recd. Aug. 16 - 1864			1st Md. Cavalry	Oct. 1861	7 July 1865 Hyperesthesia in stump	3	9
16075.	KNOTT, Edd A Morrison, Md.	176	178		F	2 Md. Inf.	19 Aug. 1861	24 Apr. 1864	2	9
16076.	BELL, Nelson Morrison, Md.	170	172 Left arm broken Battle Antietam	Sergeant	K	3 Penna Artillery	23 Oct. 1862	22 Oct. 1865 Pension applied for	3	
16077.	FULLER, Sr. Wm. H. Carney, Md.	112	114 Pectoralis Major - injured muscle	Private		Md. Vols	11 Aug. 1862	17 June 1865	2	7
16078.	EVANS, Ogden Loch Ravern, Md.	86	88 Wounded left lung	Private	D	7 Md. Vols.	17 Aug. 1862	31 May 1865	2	9
16079.	EDWARDS, Chas. Amanda Edwards, widow	65	68	Private			186	186 Papers in the hands of a pension agt.	3	
16080.	JAMES, Jno. L.	44	46	Private			186	186 Papers mislaid		

Special Schedule. Surviving Soldiers, Sailors, and Marines, and Widows, etc.

Page 2 S. D.: 1 ; E. D.: 446 ; Minor Civil Division.: 11th District

1	2	3	4	5	6	7	8	9
								Yrs Mos Dys
16081. HARRISON, Henry T. (Conf) Carney P. O., Md.	42	44					186	186 No information obtained
16082. FULLER, Jr. Wm. H. Carney P. O., Md.	246	248	Private	A	5 Md. Vols	3 Mar. 1865	close of war U. S. Wagon master Potomac Army Col. Rucket Co.	186

16083.	*SCHROEDER, Augustus R. Perry Hall, Md.	4	4				186 Volunteer wagon driver U. S. Provisions	186	
16084.	*REICHART, Philip Perry Hall, Md.	3	3				186	186	
16085.	*LOHR, Andrew Perry Hall, Md.	1	1	Sol.			186	186	

Page No. 1
Supervisor's District No. 1
Enumeration District No. 447

Eleventh Census of the United States

SPECIAL SCHEDULE
SURVIVING SOLDIERS, SAILORS, AND MARINES, AND WIDOWS, ETC.

Persons who served in the Army, Navy, and Marine Corps of the United States during the war of the rebellion (who are survivors), and widows of such persons, in   3rd Precinct 11 Dist.   , County of   Baltimore.   ,
State of   Maryland.   enumerated in June 1890

Ben. F. Taylor
Enumerator

	1	2	3	4	5	6	7	8	9
									Yrs Mos Dys
16086.	TAYLOR, Benjamin F. Bradshaw Balto., Co., Md.	1	1	Private		Vols. 2nd Maryland Veteran Shell wound left ankle gun shot wound left shoulder	Sept. 30 1861	June 16 1865 Re-enlisted veteran	3 8 16
16087.	DORSEY, Charles Bradshaw Balto., Co., Md.	7	10	Corporal	E	4 Cold. Troops Gun shot wound right side of head Gun shot wound calf of left leg	1863	1865	2
16088.	HARRIS, Asbury Bradshaw Balto., Co., Md.	29	33	Private		Cold. Troops	186	186	
16089.	TASCO, Samuel Bradshaw Balto., Co., Md.	45	49	Private		Cold. Troops	186	186	
16090.	TOODLES, Richard Upper Falls Balto., Co., Md.	33	37	Private	C	1 Cold. Troops	May 1861	1865	4
16091.	HOLTER, William H. Upper Falls Balto., Co., Md.	64	68	Private	I	26 Pa. Inft.	June 17 1863	Sept. 1863	3
16092.	JACKSON, John Mankleniville Balto., Co., Md.	94	98	Private	M	5th N. Y. H. Art.	1863	July 1865	2
16093.	CAMPBELL, John G. Mankleniville Balto., Co., Md.	97	101	Sergent	C	1 Md. Cav. Gun shot wound left side	Sept. 5 1861	Aug. 11 1865 Re enlisted veteran	3 11
16094.	JORDAN, Stephen H. Mankleniville Balto., Co., Md.	98	102	Private	F	2 Ohio Cav.	Feb. 16 1865	Aug. 11 1865	5 26
16095.	SNARE, Adam Upper Falls	115	119	Private	C	1 D. C. Inft.	June 1861	June 1864	3

16096.	BOSTICK, William Henry	129	134	Private	F	9 Md. Inft.		186	186 Also served in 1st Md. and in Navy
16097.	WILLIAMS, Frederick	138	143	Private	F	71 Pa. Inft. Wounded in the thigh Fredericksburg, Va.	July 23 1861	July	1864 3

Special Schedule. Surviving Soldiers, Sailors, and Marines, and Widows, etc.

Page 2   S. D.: 1 ; E. D.: 447   ; Minor Civil Division.: 3rd Prect. 11th Dist.

	1	2	3	4	5	6	7	8	9
									Yrs Mos Dys
16098.	MILLER, Henry Monton Balto., Co., Md.	143	139	Private	H	4th U. S. Art. Injury by being thrown by horse	Dec. 13 1864	Dec. 13 1867	3
16099.	Sarah E. Sconnion, widow of SCONNION, John Henry	150	156			Cold Troops	186	186	
16100.	BUTLER, William H. White Marsh Baltimore Co., Md.	147	153	Private	C	Dept. 9th Cold Troops	Oct. 1863	1866	
16101.	IRVIN, William M. White Marsh Baltimore Co., Md.	156	163	Private	G & K	3rd Md. Cal. Wounded in left wrist & ruptured	Sept. 18 1863	Sept. 6 1865	
16102.	Katherine Gerst, widow of GERST, Jacob Upper Falls Baltimore Co., Md.	164	171	Private		Drafted man cannot learn more	186	186	
16103.	HOBBS, William H. (Conf) Bradshaw Baltimore Co., Md.	64	68	Private			June 17 1862	Sept. 1863	
16104.	PITCOCK, Charles H.	182	189	Sergt.	H	2 Md. E. S. I.	Oct. 14 1861	July 7 1865 Enlisted in 2 Md. E. S. Infty Discharged from 2nd Md. Hy Arty	
16105.	CASSIDAY, Edward S. Jerusalem Harford Co., Md.	191	198	Private	A	9 Pa. Cal.	Sept. 14 1861	July 28 1865	
16106.	BOWEN, Frank 3rd Prect. 11 Dist.	199	206	Private		1 Col. Cav.	1863	1865	
16107.	NORWOOD, Lambert S. 3rd Prect. 11 Dist.	195	202	Private	D	1st Md. Arty	Dec. 1863	July 1865	
16108.	*CLARK, James Franklinville St.	23	26				186	186	
16109.	*BLAKENEY, Sarah widow	77	87				186	186	
16110.	*GOSNELL, Mary J. widow	86	90				186	186	

Page No. 1
Supervisor's District No. 1
Enumeration District No. 448

Eleventh Census of the United States

SPECIAL SCHEDULE
SURVIVING SOLDIERS, SAILORS, AND MARINES, AND WIDOWS, ETC

Persons who served in the Army, Navy, and Marine Corps of the United States during the war of the rebellion (who are survivors), and widows of such persons, in Highlandtown & Canton, County of Baltimore, State of Maryland, enumerated in June 1890.

John G. Hamel
Enumerator

	1	2	3	4	5	6	7	8	9		
									Yrs	Mos	Dys
16111.	KAISER, John G. 522 3rd St.			Private	A	8 D. C. Bat.	22 Apr. 1861	22 July 1861		3	
16112.	MILLER, John (Conf)			Private	H	27	22 Apr. 1861	1862			
16113.	WOLF, John 320 O'Donnell St.	102 One leg off	123	Cor.	D	4 N. Y. Cav.	18 Sept. 1861	18 Oct. 1864	3	1	
16114.	KLINE, John 424 3rd St.	424	78	Pr.	B	5 Reg. Cal.	22 Apr. 1862	23 Aug. 1863	1	4	1
16115.	ROSENTHAL, Frederick 312 Canton Ave	320 Reumtism 13 years	123	Pr.	A / B	1 Md. Art.	29 Mch 1864	3 July 1865	1	4	6
16116.	BALELKE, Fred. W. Cor. O'Donnell & Eight St.	199	242	Pr.	E	1 Md. Cal.	12 Jany 1864	12 Aug. 1865	19 m.		
16117.	STEWART, Wm. H. 16th St. Canton Ave.			Pr.	H	55 MD. Inf.	2	1862	1865	2	6
16118.	THOMPSON, George W. 16th St. Nr. Eastern Ave.			Pr.	H	11 N. Y. Cav.	Dec. 1863	Sept. 1865	2		
16119.	√THOMPSON, George W. 16th St. Nr. Eastern Ave.			Pr.	D	Dist. Col. V.	20 Apr. 1861	20 July 1861	3 m.		
16120.	MULLER, John 606 3rd St. Nr. Masson			Pr.	A	1 Md. Vol.	16 Aug. 1861	20 Oct. 1862	1	2	

Page No. 1
Supervisor's District No. 1
Enumeration District No. 449

Eleventh Census of the United States

SPECIAL SCHEDULE
SURVIVING SOLDIERS, SAILORS, AND MARINES, AND WIDOWS, ETC.

Persons who served in the Army, Navy, and Marine Corps of the United States during the war of the rebellion (who are survivors), and widows of such persons, in 1st Prect. 12th Dis., County of Baltimore, State of Maryland, enumerated in June 1890.

George W. Keen

Enumerator

	1	2	3	4	5	6	7	8	9 Yrs Mos Dys
16121.	SCHMIDT, George 24 No. 28 Elliot St. Balto., Co., Md.			Corporal None	F	1 Md. Cav.	1 Oct. 1861	8 Aug. 186	3 10 7
16122.	UNDERWOOD, James No. 21 O'Donnell Balto., Co., Md.			Private None	C	3 Md. Inf.	1863	1865	3
16123.	JOHN, David B. No. 5 Ponca St. Balto., Co., Md.			Fireman None		Vessel Octorora	15 Aug. 1862	18 Aug. 1863	1 0 3
16124.	William T. Jenkins McBUKOFFSKY, George H. No. 256 Clinton St. Balto., Co., Md.			Fireman Fireman None		Vessel Octorora Vessel Shamokin	15 Aug. 1862 10 May 1865	18 Aug. 1863 10 Mar. 1868	2 10
16125.	WYMAN, Joseph A. No. 316 First St. Balto., Co., Md.			Corporal Toe cut off by artillery wagon		Alexander Bat.	Aug. 1862	June 1865	2 10
16126.	SAUER, Charles C. No. 104 First St. Baltimore Co., Md			Seaman Landsman None		U. S. Ship Sawonee U. S. Ship Vermont	2 Mar. 1865	5 April 1867	2 1 3
16127.	MORGAN, George W. No. 205 Clinton St. Baltimore Co., Md.			Corporal Gun Shot wounded at Battle of Bull Run	I	2 Md. Vols.	10 July 1861	23 Dec. 1862 Discharge after Battle of Bull Run	1 5 13
16128.	DANNENFELSER, George 43 Clinton St. Baltimore Co., Md.			Landsman None		Minnesota	5 Aug. 1864	June 1865	10
16129.	√CRONE, Jacob 37 Clinton St. Baltimore Co., Md.			None			186	186 Lost papers	
16130.	EVANS, David 19 Clinton St. Baltimore Co., Md.			Private None	F	1 Md. Cav.	9 Feb. 1864	8 Aug. 1865	5 30

Special Schedule. Surviving Soldiers, Sailors, and Marines, and Widows, etc.

Page 2   S. D.: 1 ; E. D.: 449 ; Minor Civil Division.:

	1	2	3	4	5	6	7	8	9 Yrs Mos Dys
16131.	CROCKETT, Andrew J. First 213 Baltimore Co., Md.			Private		9 Md. Inf.	19 June 1863 Enlisted as private dis. as Corporal 1 Md. Art.	24 June 1865	2 0 5
16132.	EDWARDS, David First 217 Baltimore Co., Md.						186 Lost papers	186	
16133.	Elizabeth Edwards, widow of LEWIS, Henry First 203 Baltimore Co., Md.			Private	D	1 Md. Inf.	23 Mar. 1864	24 June 1865	1 3 1

No.	Name	Rank	Co.	Regiment	Enlisted	Discharged	Yrs	Mos	Dys
16134.	HOLBROOK, John H. 3 1st Ave. Balto., Co., Md. Wounded at Bat. of Wilderness	Captain	H	2 Mich. Inf.	14 April 1861	14 Feb. 1865	3	10	
16135.	JANNUSCH, William 17 1st Ave. Balto., Co., Md.	Seaman		Paul Jones	22 April 1862	9 May 1865	3		17
16136.	THORN, Charles A. 236 Clinton St. Balto., Co., Md.				186	186 Could not obtain any information			
16137.	HUBER, Antoine 322 Clinton St. Balto., Co., Md. Wounded in thigh	Sergent	K	5 Md. Reg.	186	186 Could not obtain any information			
16138.	DOSCH, Andrew 408 Clinton St. Balto., Co., Md.	Sergent	L	1 Md. Reg. Flesh wound	8 Aug. 1861	8 Aug. 1865	4	0	0
16139.	DOWDERS, John F. 410 Clinton St. Balto., Co., Md.	Private	B	1 Md. Reg.	8 Aug. 1861	8 Aug. 1864	3	0	0
16140.	Annie M. Sowders, widow of CULVER, Charles B. 408 Clinton St. Balto., Co., Md.	Engineer Wounded in right eye		Com. Barney	14 Jan. 1863	26 Sep. 1865 Lost sight of right eye from smallpox	1	8	12
16141.	VOLLMER, John A. Baltimore Co., Md.	Private	K	1 U. S. Artl.	16 Aug. 1858	16 Aug. 1863	5	0	0
16142.	HATTON, George J. Proctor P. O. Baltimore Co., Md.	Private	K	3 Md. Cav.	9 Oct. 1863	7 Sept. 1865	1	10	29
16143.	CHANDLER, William E. Proctor P. O. Baltimore Co., Md.	Private	A	1 Md. Cav.	29 Sep. 1861	29 Sep. 1864	3	0	0
16144.	SMITH, Henry A. Proctor P. O. Baltimore Co., Md.	Private	B	1 Md. Art.	6 Oct. 1864	3 July 1865		9	

Special Schedule. Surviving Soldiers, Sailors, and Marines, and Widows, etc.

Page

S. D.:   ; E. D.:   ; Minor Civil Division.:

1	2	3	4	5	6	7	8	9
								Yrs Mos Dys
16145. PAUL, George W. (Conf) 42 Clinton St. Balto., Co., Md.			Private	H	1 Vir. Inf.	17 April 1861	17 April 1865	4 0 0
16146. SCHMIDT, John (Conf) 317 O'Donnell St. Balto., Co., Md.			Private	E	12 Vir. Cav.	15 May 1862	19 April 1865	3 11 4
16147. BROWN, Magnus (Conf) 322 Clinton St. Balto., Co., Md.			Private	D	1 S. C. Inf.	Dec. 1859	Aug. 1863	3 8 0
16148. BUCK, John H. (Conf) 219 Clinton St. Balto., Co., Md.						186	186	

Eleventh Census of the United States

Supervisor's District No. 1
Enumeration District No. 450

SPECIAL SCHEDULE
SURVIVING SOLDIERS, SAILORS, AND MARINES, AND WIDOWS, ETC.

Persons who served in the Army, Navy, and Marine Corps of the United States during the war of the rebellion (who are survivors), and widows of such persons, in 1st Precinct 12 Dist. , County of Baltimore.
State of Maryland. enumerated in June 1890

George H. Garratt
Enumerator

	1	2	3	4	5	6	7	8	9		
									Yrs	Mos	Dys
16149.	BUETTNER, Edward 802 Clinton St.	10	16	Private	C	9 Inft.	27 Feb. 186	26 Feb. 1867	3		
16150.	WILLIAMS, August 818 Clinton St.	18	28	Private Shot in hand Jan. 1865	E	4th U. S. Artil	Re-enlisted 6 Feb. 1864 June 1861	8 Aug. 1865 5 Feb. 186	1 2	7 7	0 0
16151.	JENKINS, William 814 Clinton St.	16	25	Private 1861 sickness from exposure	C	3rd Pa. Artillery	don't know date 1861	186	0	3	0
16152.	HARRIS, John T. col. 844 Clinton St.	24	35	Private Bayonet run through knee	A	Col. Troops 3 Reg. U. S.	26 June 1863	31 Oct. 1865	2	4	0
16153.	HOPKINS, Moses col. 1027 Clinton St.	36	49	Private Shot in side & leg	A	5 Mass. Calavry	15 Apr. 1863	Apr. 1865	2	0	0
16154.	DEXTER, Samuel 11th Ave. Lower Canton	43	58	Corporal	C	Artillery 6 N. Y. Heavy	28 March 1863	24 Aug. 1865	2	5	0
16155.	HOFFMAN, Charles 107 First St. - Lower Canton	44	59	Sergeant	E	2 Md. Vol. Inft.	1 Jan. 1864	17 July 1865	1	6	17
16156.	FLYNN, John 107 First St. - Lower Canton	68	83	Private	C	Artillery 5 N. Y. Heavy	Jan. 1863	June 1865	1	8	
16157.	alias Tully SPANGLEY, Andrew 99 First St. & 8th Ave. Canton	71	87	Private		103 Penn. Vol.	8 March 1865	25 June 1865		4	17
16158.	HENRY, John 203 8th Ave. Lower Canton	73	89	Fireman		Flag Ship Malven	drafted 1861	discharged at fall of 186	Richmond		
16159.	ONSSEN, James 203 8th Ave. Lower Canton	73	90	Quarter Master		Monongahala	186	186			
16160.	BURRIER, Solomon 14th St. Balto., Co., Md.	86	110	Private Gun shot wound & piles also deafness & dizziness	F	5 Md. Inft.	16 Dec. 1861	1 Sept. 1865	3	9	

Special Schedule. Surviving Soldiers, Sailors, and Marines, and Widows, etc.

Page

S. D.:   ; E. D.:   ; Minor Civil Division.:

1	2	3	4	5	6	7	8	9
								Yrs Mos Dys
Martha A. Potter, widow of 16161. BOOTMAN, John W. Canton P. Office	90	115	Cook		Ship Constellation	1861	Jan. 1865 Papers lost	
16162. SIMS, George B.	91	116	Private	B	Battery B	1861	1864 Reinlisted Battery B, Md. Art. 6 months	
William Harding (alias) 16163. BRYSON, Ferdmand R. Canton P. Office	91	116	Private Disability - kidney	B	1st Dist. Washington	14 Oct. 1862	21 July 1866	
16164. FALCK, William C. Point Breeze Hotel	93	119	Private			186	186	
16165. PAYNE, Travers 8th Ave. Lower Canton	75	95	Corporal Shot above knee cap	G	1st Conn. Battalion	7 May 1863	Oct. 1865	
16166. SAUTRE, Jacob F. (Conf)	5	9				186	186	

Page No. 1
Supervisor's District No. 1
Enumeration District No. 451

Eleventh Census of the United States

SPECIAL SCHEDULE
SURVIVING SOLDIERS, SAILORS, AND MARINES, AND WIDOWS, ETC.

Persons who served in the Army, Navy, and Marine Corps of the United States during the war of the rebellion (who are survivors), and widows of such persons, in   2nd Pre. 12th District   , County of   Baltimore.   ,
State of   Maryland.   enumerated in June 1890

John H. S. Clarke
Enumerator

1	2	3	4	5	6	7	8	9
								Yrs Mos Dys
16167. SCHMUCK, Henry Rosedale Balto., Co., Md.	19	20	Private	H	5th Md. V. V.	Oct. 11 1864	Sep. 1 1865	10 20
16168. SEIF, Martin Rosedale Balto., Co., Md.	17	18	Private	D	8 Md. V. Inf.	May 1862 Dis. filed pension office	May 1865	3
16169. KURTZ, Henry Rosedale Balto., Co., Md.	30	31	Private	K	73 Pa. Vol. Inf.	May 1861	June 1862	1 1 13
16170. JOHNSON, John Rosedale Balto., Co., Md.	36	37	Private	C	Transf. 36 Mass. Vet. Vol.	1862 1863 Dis. mislaid	1865	2 6

Page -77-

No.	Name			Rank	Co.	Regiment	Enlisted	Discharged	Yrs	Mos	Dys
16171.	SCHENKEL, Leonard Golden Ring Balto., Co., Md.	82	86	Corporal	A	3rd Md. Vet. Batta Div.	Nov. 16 1861 Dec. 29 1863	Nov. 17 1863 July 31 1865 Reinlisted Dec. 29th 1863 same Regiment	3	8	14
16172.	THOMSON, Thomas Chase Balto., Co., Md.	107	112	Private	K	2nd Md. Vol. V.	July 17 1863	July 2 1865 Transferred from Pernel L. to 2nd Md.	1	11	15
16173.	George A. Porter, alias SEAGER, George Chase Balto., Co., Md.	108	113	Private	B	1st Md. Cav. Vol.	Nov. 11 1864	Aug. 8 1865 Inlisted under name of George Seager	1	4	27
16174.	HOPKINS, Alfred T. Chase Balto., Co., Md.	112	117	Private	B	5th Md. Vet. Vol.	Oct. 5 1863	Sep. 15 1865	3	11	10
16175.	UNDERWOOD, Elijah Chase Balto., Co., Md.	134	142	Private	K	34th U.S. Vol.	1864	1864 Discharge papers given to C. Agt. & lost ingalh to give exact dates (col)			
16176.	DEBRULER, James E. Chase Balto., Co., Md.	136	144	Private He left service because he was not Furnished with horse	H	Hav. Batt. Coles 1st Potom.	Feb. 25 1864	Aug. 1864 In 8th Cav. May 1, 1864 at Pro. Sergant deserted & doesnt know exact dates	5		
16177.	SKINNER, John B. Rossville Balto. Co., Md.	180	188	Corporal Had sun stroke & rhumatism	I	4th Wis. Cav.	May 28 1861	Dec. 31 1863 Served 2 terms hence unreadable	2	8	3
16178.	√ SKINNER, John B. Rossville Balto., Co., Md.	180	188	Artificer Causing slight defective hearing & sight him 2 spaces	I	4th Wis. Cav.	Jan. 1 1864	Aug. 19 1865	1	7	18

Special Schedule. Surviving Soldiers, Sailors, and Marines, and Widows, etc.

Page no 2   S. D.: 1 ; E. D.: 451   ; Minor Civil Division.: 2 Precinct 12th District

1	2	3	4	5	6	7	8	9
								Yrs Mos Dys
16179. LEE, William H. (col) Rossville Balto., Co., Md.	184	192					186	186 Could not see the person and I was unable to get information
16180. Johanna Nollert, widow of NOLBERT, George Rosedale Balto., Co., Md.	18	19	He died while in the service				186	186 Died in service widow is a pensioner
16181. Virginia E. Taylor, widow of TAYLOR, Harrison Rosedale Balto., Co., Md.	14	15					186	186 Refused to give particulars, get pension

Eleventh Census of the United States

SPECIAL SCHEDULE

SURVIVING SOLDIERS, SAILORS, AND MARINES, AND WIDOWS, ETC.

Persons who served in the Army, Navy, and Marine Corps of the United States during the war of the rebellion (who are survivors), and

widows of such persons, in   12th District   , County of   Baltimore.
State of   Maryland.   enumerated in June 1890

Joseph H. Volz
Enumerator

1	2	3	4	5	6	7	8	9
								Yrs Mos Dys
16182. ASHER, James H. Rossville, Md.	5	5		C	11 Maryland	drafted 1862	Dec. 1862	30
16183. WHITEFORD, John S. Stag Balto., Co., Md.			Private	C	Pennsylvania	1862	Aug. 1865	3 4
16184. HILL William H. c/o John W. Ford 2110 E. Pratt St. Baltimore, Md.			Union Srage.		Mexican war	186	186	
16185. JOHNSON, Henry Rossville, Md.			Private	B	23 Dist. Columbia	1863	1865	2 6
16186. HOWE, George Rossville, Md.			Private Afflicted in hip by marching	C	54 Arkansas	1863	1866	3
16187. PASTERS, James T. Rossville, Md.			Private	B	5 Maryland	1861	1865	4 2
16188. MYERS, Charles Rossville, Md.						186	186	
16189. JORDON, Henry Rossville, Md.			Private 3 fingers mashed off	C	11 Tennessee	1864	1865 1 One finger now missing	
16190. LENNING, John Rossville, Md.			Private	A	2 Dist. Colubia	1861	1861	4
16191. ROAT, John Rossville, Md.			Private	A	1 Charleston S. C.	1861	1862 1	
16192. SIMMS, Thomas Rossville, Md.			Private	H	4 New Jersey	1864	1865	6
16193. FORD, Charles H. Rossville, Md.			Private	A	1 Maryland	1861	1865	4 4

Special Schedule. Surviving Soldiers, Sailors, and Marines, and Widows, etc.
Page

S. D.:   ; E. D.:   452   ; Minor Civil Division.:   12th District

1	2	3	4	5	6	7	8	9
								Yrs Mos Dys
16194. RHODES, Thomas A. Rossville, Md.			Private		New York	1861	1865	4

Page -79-

No.	Name	Notes	Rank	Co.	Regiment	Enlisted	Discharged	Yrs	Mos
16195.	AHLEE, John Rossville, Md.		Private		Mexican war	186	186		
16196.	STATEN, Jeremiah Rossville, Md.		Private			1862	1865	3	
16197.	MADDOX, William E. Triumph, Md.	Stabed in side by comrade	Private	A	1 Maryland	1864	1865 Suffering now from rhumatism	1	
16198.	JACKSON, Thomas Triumph, Md.		Private	C	2 Indiana	1864	1865	1	5
16199.	YOUNG, John Triumph, Md.		Private	G	7 Maryland	1863	1866	3	3
16200.	MADDOX, John J. Triumph, Md.		Private	A	1 Maryland	1864	1865	1	
16201.	PRESTON, Henry Triumph, Md.		Private	K	30 Maryland	1864	June 30 1865 Dec.	1	6
16202.	HEGEMAN, Henry Rossville, Md.	Shot in right knee	Seargeant	A	45 New York	Oct. 1861	1865 Now suffering from rhumatism	4	
16203.	GREEN, Thomas Chase, Md.		Private	A	8 Pennsylvania	1862	1865	3	
16204.	PRESTON, Thomas Chase, Md.		Private			186	186		
16205.	PITTS, Henry C. Triumph, Md.		Private	F	30 Maryland	June 1864	Dec. 1865	1	6
16206.	ECCLESTON, James H. Chase, Md.		Private			1866 Ruptured	1868	3	
16207.	NEWKIRK, Joseph V. (Conf) Chase, Md.	Shot in left thy	Private	E	1 Maryland	Sept. 1863	June 1865	2	

Special Schedule. Surviving Soldiers, Sailors, and Marines, and Widows, etc.

Page

S. D.: ; E. D.: 452 ; Minor Civil Division.: 12th District

1	2	3	4	5	6	7	8	9
								Yrs Mos Dys
16208. SCOTT, Jocuvus Chase			Cook				1862	1865
16209. LOUIS, Henry Chase			Private	C	19 Maryland		1865	1865 0
16210. DICKSON, James							186	186

16211.	*McCLELLAND, John T. 12 District	126	126	Private			186	186
16212.	*MILLS, Robert 12 District	105	105	Private			186	186
16213.	*TAYLOR, William J. 12 District	95	95	Private			186	186
16214.	*THOMAS, Jackson 12 District	92	92	Private			186	186

Page No.
Supervisor's District No. 1
Enumeration District No. 453

Eleventh Census of the United States

SPECIAL SCHEDULE
SURVIVING SOLDIERS, SAILORS, AND MARINES, AND WIDOWS, ETC.

Persons who served in the Army, Navy, and Marine Corps of the United States during the war of the rebellion (who are survivors), and widows of such persons, in   3rd Precinct 1st District   , County of   Baltimore.
State of   Maryland.   enumerated in June 1890

Alexander W. McCormick Jr.
Enumerator

1	2	3	4	5	6	7	8	9
								Yrs Mos Dys
16215. SEABOLD, George W. Parkville Balto., Co., Md.			Private Prisoner at Lby prison 2 months Bell Island 2 months	Light Baltimore Art.	Md. Bat.	9 Aug. 1862	17 June 1865 Neuralgia & rhumatism (disabled)	3 3 8
16216. HOOK, William Parkville Balto., Co., Md.			Corporal Wounded in head	B	2 U. S. Reg.	4 June 1864	29 Sept. 1864	3
16217. √HOOK, William Parkville Balto., Co., Md.			Private	I	9 U. S. Inft.	10 May 1865	1860	5
16218. √HOOK, William Parkville Balto., Co., Md.			Corporal	B	U. S. Inf.	1845	1848	3
16219. BADER, John Parkville Balto., Co., Md.			Private	A	1 Md. Reg.	5 Oct. 1864	4 July 1865 Inflamitory rhumatism	11
(B) 16220. DECKERD, Frederick J. Lauraville Baltimore Co., Md.			Private	D	4 Md. Reg.	Apl 1861	1861 3 years driving ambulance	6
16221. GATCH, Thomas B (Cof) Gardenville Baltimore Co.	Sol.		Capt. Wounded 5 times 9 months in Ft. Delaware	G	Davis Cavalry Cav.	21 June 1861	21 June 1865	4
16222. RASP, John H. Lauraville Baltimore Co.			Government Construction Train Md. Le wounded & ruptured	G	Engineer Sneed Capt. Rosell	Sept. 1863	1865 Went in as Private came out Corporal	1 4

	1	2	3	4	5	6	7	8	9		
									Yrs	Mos	Dys
16223.	ROSENBERGER, Louis Lauraville Balto., Co., Md.			Private Corporal None	A	Md. Reg.	11 Aug. 1862	13 June 1865	2	9	28
16224.	John C. Evans alias SMITH, John T. Gardenville, P. O. Balto., Co., Md.			Private None	H	15 N. Y. Reg. Went in as a Private and promoted to Corporal	1864	1865	1	4	
16225.	Ellen J. Kahler, widow of KAHLER, William Gardenville Balto., Co., Md.			Private None		Engineer Sneed Capt. Rosell	Sept. 1863	1865	1	4	
16226.	KOPPLEMAN, John H. Gardenville Baltimore Co., Md.			Govt. contractor or engineer Sneed Train Enginer Corp None		Capt. Rosell	1863	1865	1	4	

Special Schedule. Surviving Soldiers, Sailors, and Marines, and Widows, etc.

Page

S. D.:   ; E. D.:   ; Minor Civil Division.:

	1	2	3	4	5	6	7	8	9		
									Yrs	Mos	Dys
16227.	ELLINGSON, Julius Rosedale Balto., Co., Md.			Private Wounded in leg	K	2nd Md. Reg. Inf.	24 Aug. 1861	24 Aug. 1864	3		
16228.	ESDON, William R. Gardenville Baltimore Co.			Private	A	1st Minnesota Reg	29 Apl 1861	8 Nov. 186	7		
16229.	EHRHARDT, George Gardenville Baltimore Co., Md.			Private Sabre wound in hand		Frigate Congress Brooklyn N. Y.	186	186 Also was in Mexican war in 1845 he has lost his papers	4		
16230.	*DUVALL, George W. 3rd Precinct Baltimore Co.	58	58				186	186			

Page No. 1
Supervisor's District No. 1 Md.
Enumeration District No. 454

Eleventh Census of the United States

SPECIAL SCHEDULE
SURVIVING SOLDIERS, SAILORS, AND MARINES, AND WIDOWS, ETC.

Persons who served in the Army, Navy, and Marine Corps of the United States during the war of the rebellion (who are survivors), and widows of such persons, in   4th Prect 12 District   , County of   Baltimore.   ,
State of   Maryland.   enumerated in June 1890

C. Ross Mace
Enumerator

	1	2	3	4	5	6	7	8	9		
									Yrs	Mos	Dys
16231.	DUMER, August Fullerton Balto., Co., Md.	12	13	Sergeant Kicked by mule when on duty	A	2 U. S. H. A.	21 Aug. 1860	15 July 1867	6	10	24

Page -82-

16232.	PHENIS, Charles 31	32	Private	G	75 Pa. Inf.	23 Sept. 1861	Aug. 1863	1	10
	Fullerton Balto., Co., Md.		None						
16233.	CHENWORTH, John T. 67	72	Sergant	D	7 Md. Inf.	21 Aug. 1862	June 1865	2	10
	Parkville Balto., Co., Md.		None						
16234.	LAW, John H. 158	165	Private	A	1 Pa. Resr.	28 Apr. 1861	June 1864	3	3
	Necker Balto., Co., Md.		Wounded in left knee & rt. shoulder						
16235.	DECKMAN, Peter W. 163	170	Sergant	B	4 D. C. Inf.	7 Aug. 1862	3 June 1865	2	10
	Rossville Balto., Co., Md.		Chronic diarrhoea						

Page No.
Supervisor's District No. 1
Enumeration District No. 455-a

Eleventh Census of the United States

SPECIAL SCHEDULE
SURVIVING SOLDIERS, SAILORS, AND MARINES, AND WIDOWS, ETC.

Persons who served in the Army, Navy, and Marine Corps of the United States during the war of the rebellion (who are survivors), and widows of such persons, in   5th Pre. 12th Dist.   , County of   Baltimore.
State of   Maryland.   enumerated in June 1890

Alexander McCormick Jr.
Enumerator

1	2	3	4	5	6	7	8	9
								Yrs Mos Dys
16236. EXTINE, George			Private		15th Iowa Reg.	Nov. 1864	Sept. 1865	10
Rosedale Balto., Co., Md.								
16237. CUNNINGHAM, Aquilla			Private		3 Md. Pernell Legion	18 Aug. 1861	24 Oct. 1864	3
Rosedale Baltimore Co., Md.							Was promoted to Sargent after 1st year	

Page No. 1
Supervisor's District No. 1
Enumeration District No. 455

Eleventh Census of the United States

SPECIAL SCHEDULE
SURVIVING SOLDIERS, SAILORS, AND MARINES, AND WIDOWS, ETC.

Persons who served in the Army, Navy, and Marine Corps of the United States during the war of the rebellion (who are survivors), and widows of such persons, in   Prec. 5; Dist. 12   , County of   Baltimore.
State of   Maryland.   enumerated in June 1890

Joseph German
Enumerator

1	2	3	4	5	6	7	8	9
								Yrs Mos Dys
					Purnell Legion Infantry			
16238. NORRIS, Richard S. 30		31	Private	A	7 Md. Vols.	Oct. 8 1861	Oct. 24 1864	3 3
Baltimore, 77 E. Monument St.			Wounded by a shell				Laid up in hospital	
16239. KLENGSTEIN, Charles 36		37	Private	B	22nd Penna. Cavalry	Oct. 1862	186	3
1st Toll Gate Belair Road			None				Discharge papers lost	

16240.	MAGNESS, Thomas M. Orangeville	57	59	Private	A	Infantry 1st Md. Reg. Wounded 4 times	May 10 1861	May 10 1864 In hospital nearly 1 yr	3		
16241.	SKIPPER, George W. Baltimore, Maryland	64	66	Private	I	5 Md. Infty Rheumatism from exposure	Feb. 22 1864	Sep. 1 1865	1	6	9
16242.	FISHER, Thomas A. Baltimore	69	71	Private	A	10 Md. Infty	June 18 1861	Jan. 9 1864	2	6	21
16243.	Mary A. Jett, widow of RYNE, Hamilton Orangeville	81	83	Private	G	6th E. Tess. Infty Wounded in Mexican War	Apr. 14 1862	May 17 1865	4	1	3
16244.	FORD, John H. Orangeville	82	84	Private	E	121 Pa. Vols. Bullet wound in face	Aug. 18 1862	July 3 1865 About 14 months in hospital	2	10	15
16245.	BRATT, James E. Baltimore	83	85	Private None	D	Battery 1st Md. Light Arty	Feb. 16 1864	Jan. 14 1865 Nose broken while in service	1	3	28
16246.	TAYLOR, Charles A. Highlandtown	121	143	Private None	B	9th Reg. Md. Infty	June 20 1863	Feb. 23 1864 Contracted rheumatism		8	3
16247.	ROSS, George H. Highlandtown	144	164	Corporal		Alleghany Ruptured, kidney disease & rheumatism contracted in service	July 18 1866	July 18 1867	4		
16248.	HARTLEY, John R. Baltimore	157	177	Private	B	Battery reenlisted in 1st Md.	1862	1865	2	6	
16249.	HEUER, Frederick W. Baltimore	172	195	Private			186	186			

Special Schedule. Surviving Soldiers, Sailors, and Marines, and Widows, etc.

Page 2   S. D.: 1   ; E. D.: 455   ; Minor Civil Division.:   Md.

1	2	3	4	5	6	7	8	9
								Yrs Mos Dys
16250. WALTJEN, Andrew S. Baltimore	180 155	203 179	Private	B	143 Pa. Reg.		186 Papers not present	186 3 3
16251. MILLER, John B. Baltimore	194	217	Private		1st Pa. Vols.	July 1864	Dec. 1864 Papers sent to Washington	4
16252. JONES, J. Wymne Baltimore	154	174	Private 13th Army Corps 1st Brigade 4th D.	G	Wis. Infty 23 Reg. Volls.	Aug. 14 1862	July 4 1865 Private, Corporal & Sergeant	2 10 20
16253. Sarah O'Dell, widow of O'DELL, Daniel Baltimore	199	223			has not the papers of husband		186	186

No.	Name & Address			Rank	Co.	Regiment/Vessel	Enlisted	Discharged	Yrs	Mos	Dys
16254.	MILLER, Joseph M. Baltimore	197	220	Private Heart disease	K	101 Pa. Vols.	Dec. 28 1861	June 27 1863	1	5	29
16255.	LOGAN, Francis 201 Clairmount Ave. Highland Town Balto., Co., Md.	207 183	233 208	Corporal	A	8 Md. Vols.	Aug. 13 1862	May 31 1865	2	9	18
16256.	HEIKEL, John 3104 3rd Ave. Highland Town Balto., Co., Md.	212 184	239 215	Private		Mystic - vessel	1864	1865		11	
16257.	SEALOVER, Asher Highland Town cor. Pratt & 3rd Str.	222	253	Private Wounded twice	A	122 Ohio Vols.	Aug. 22 1865	1865			
16258.	KANE, Andrew J. Sparrows Point Balto., Co., Md.	222	253	Private Disabled in right ankle & chroinc diarrhea during the war	H	203 Pa. Vols.	Sep. 2 1864	June 22 1865		9	20
16259.	RAAB, George 422 Eastern Ave. Highland Town	301	344	Private Contracted rheumatisn in service	G	3rd P. H. B.	Feb. 15 1865	May 29 1865		3	14
16260.	STUMMER, William Baltimore	41	42	Defective mind from the firing of canon			186	186			
16261.	KELLY, Edward	59	61				186	186			
16262.	BOND, William Orangeville	367	396	3rd Asst.	Eng.	U. S. Navy	June 23 1863	May 27 1867	3	11	4
16263.	GROSKAPF, George 817 Lombard St., Extended Highland Town Balto., Co., Md.	360	409	Private Wounded in the head	K	1st Md. Infty	Jan. 6 1865	July 2 1865 Which has produced continous headaches	5	8	

Special Schedule. Surviving Soldiers, Sailors, and Marines, and Widows, etc.

Page

S. D.: 1 ; E. D.: 455 ; Minor Civil Division.: Prect. 5 Dist. 12 Md. 3

	1	2	3	4	5	6	7	8	9		
									Yrs	Mos	Dys
16264.	FUNCK, David Orangeville Balto., Co.	377	428	Private	B	6th Md. Vols.	June 25 1863	Jan. 16 1864		6	21
16265.	JANEY, Doct. E. W. Highlandtown Balto., Co.	156	176	Acting (U. S.) Asst.		Contract Surgeon	1863	to 1867	3		
16266.	RICHARDS, Henry S. Highlandtown Balto., Co.	203	229	Private	I	76 Pa. Vols.	Mar. 1 1864	July 18 1865	1	4	17
16267.	FORD, William G.	13	13				186	186			

16268. BUTTON, James O. Highlandtown	116	116				186	186	
16269. ABBOTT, Charles C. Orangeville Balto., Co.	357	406				186	186	
16270. BRATT, Samuel J. Highlandtown	397	449				186	186	
16271. REDING, John W. Highlandtown Eastern Ave.	291	330 Rheumatism 20 yrs			U. S. Marine	186	186	

Special Schedule. Surviving Soldiers, Sailors, and Marines, and Widows, etc.

Page

S. D.:   1   ; E. D.:   455   ; Minor Civil Division.:

1	2	3	4	5	6	7	8	9
								Yrs Mos Dys
16272. *WHITE, Nathan Phila. Road Balto., Md.	365	416				186	186	

Note:-The provision of the act of March 1, 1889, under which this special enumeration of survivors of the war of the rebellion is made, reads as follows:

That said Superintendent shall under the authority of the Secretary of the Interior, cause to be taken on a special schedule of inquiry, according to such form as he may prescribe, the names, organizations, and length of service of those who had served in the Army, Navy, or Marines Corps of the United States in the war of the rebellion, and who are survivors at the time of said inquiry, and the widows of soldiers, sailors, or marines.

The entries concerning each survivor or widow should be carefully and accurately made, so that the printed reports may contain only thoroughly trustworthy information.

Spaces are provided on this special schedule for the entry of fifty names, or more properly, term of service. The spaces are numbered consecutively from 1 to 50, and cover the four pages comprised in each schedule. The inquiries made concerning each survivor or widow call for the repetition of the number of the house and family as returned on the general population schedule (No. 1), the name, rank company, regiment or vessel, date of enlistment, date of discharge, and length of service (in years, months, and days) on the upper half of each page, and the post-office address, disability incurred, and general remarks on the lower half of each page. The column headed "Remarks" is intended to be used to cover any points not included in the forgoing inquires, and which are necessary to a complete statement of a person's term of service in any one organization.

In the case of persons having served in more than one organization, use as many spaces as may be necessary to cover their various terms of service. In the case of widows of deceased soldiers, sailors, or marines, make the entry of her name on the dotted lines, as follows: Mary J., widow of filling out the record of his service during the war, and giving under "post-office address" the Present address of his widow.   BROWN, James H.

Page No.
Supervisor's District No. 1
Enumeration District No. 456

Eleventh Census of the United States

SPECIAL SCHEDULE
SURVIVING SOLDIERS, SAILORS, AND MARINES, AND WIDOWS, ETC.

Persons who served in the Army, Navy, and Marine Corps of the United States during the war of the rebellion (who are survivors), and widows of such persons, in   Sparrows Point   , County of   Baltimore.
State of   Maryland.   enumerated in June 1890

Campion Rush
Enumerator

1	2	3	4	5	6	7	8	9
								Yrs Mos Dys

16273.	GREEN, Thomas Sparrows Point	49			Purnell Legion	Mar. 14 1861	Mar. 1865 Transferred to 1st Maryland	4	
16274.	WEBSTER, John W. Sparrows Point	Malarial poisoning			136 New York		1862	Jan. 1 1863	1
16275.	SMITH, Peter Sparrow Point	Chronic diarrhea					1862	1865	3
16276.	JOHNSON, Jeff Sparrow Point				32nd Pennsylvania	Feb. 1864	Nov. 1865	2	9
16277.	COLEMAN, James H. Sparrow Point			Drum Sergt.	5 Mass.	Mch 1863	Apr. 1865	2	1
16278.	HESLEY, Menie widow Sparrow Point	26			1st Md. Infantry	186 Draws pension	186		
16279.	SCHUNCK, Robert Sparrow Point	Rheumatism			Monticello	1861 Pension applied for	Feb. 1862	1	
16280.	√SCHUNCK, Robert North Point	Hip out of joint			1st P. H. B. Md.	186	186		
16281.	KEYES, Walter Sparrow Point			Private	2nd Maryland	Feb. 1861	Feb. 1864		
16282.	*GARRISH, William H. North Point	68	68			186	186		
16283.	*SCOTT, George W.	89	89			186	186		
16284.	*JUBB, Richard	98	98			186	186		

Special Schedule. Surviving Soldiers, Sailors, and Marines, and Widows, etc.

Page

S. D.: 1 ; E. D.: 456 ; Minor Civil Division.: Maryland

1	2	3	4	5	6	7	8	9
								Yrs Mos Dys
16285. *BARNES, George W. Sparrows Point, Md.	109	109				186	186	
16286. *KUHL, Leonard North Point, Md.	96	96				186	186	
16287. *HUMPHREYS, Edward North Point, Md.	96	96				186	186	
16288. *HALLAM, William North Point, Md.	96	96				186	186	

	1	2	3	4	5	6	7	8	9
16289.	*SMITH, Peter Sparrows Point, Md.	53	53					186	186

Eleventh Census of the United States

Page No 1
Supervisor's District No. 1
Enumeration District No. 456-a

SPECIAL SCHEDULE
SURVIVING SOLDIERS, SAILORS, AND MARINES, AND WIDOWS, ETC.

Persons who served in the Army, Navy, and Marine Corps of the United States during the war of the rebellion (who are survivors), and widows of such persons, in Sparrows Point, County of Baltimore, State of Maryland, enumerated in July 1890

W. D. McCork
Enumerator

	1	2	3	4	5	6	7	8	9 Yrs Mos Dys
16290.	CODER, John G. 1 West E. St.	1	1				186	186 Could not obtain information	
16291.	MYERS, Harry 23 West E. St.	11	12	Private	A	77 Pa. Inf.	Apr. 6 1865	Oct. 6 1866	
16292.	COLEMAN, Levi 23 West E. St.	11	12	Priv.	K D	166 Pa. Inf. 202 Pa. Inf.	Nov. 9 1862 Aug. 31 1864	July 28 1863 Aug. 3 1865	
16293.	McCROSKY, James A. 4 E. St. West	24	28	Priv.	D	47 Pa. Inf.	Aug. 10 1861	Jan. 10 1866	5
16294.	SHRIVER, Alexander 20 West E. St.	32	36	Priv.	E	12 Pa. Cav.	Mar. 5 1864	July 20 1865	
16295.	McGOWAN, James 19 West F. St.	56	61				186	186 Could not obtain information	
16296.	BRENEMAN, Christian 23 West F. St.	58	63				186	186 Could not obtain information	
16297.	HILDERBRANDT, Cheek 25 West F. St.	59	64				186	186 Out of town cant find out	
16298.	McCLEARY, Nelson 27 West F. St.	60	65	Private	A	21 Pa. Cav.	Sept. 1863	July 17 1865	
16299.	MARTIN, William 43 West F. St.	68	74				186	186 Cant get information	
16300.	WALLS, Charles 47 West F. St.	70	76	Private	H	61 Pa. Inf.	Sept. 4 1861	Sept. 4 1864	3 0 0
16301.	DEVINNEY, Jeremiah 2 West F. St.	71	77	Private			186	186 Cant get information	

Special Schedule. Surviving Soldiers, Sailors, and Marines, and Widows, etc.

Page 2 ; S. D.: 1 ; E. D.: 456-a ; Minor Civil Division.: Maryland

	1	2	3	4	5	6	7	8	9 Yrs Mos Dys
16302.	STAUBER, George 40 West F. St.	89	95				186	186 Cant get information	
16303.	SNAVELY, Henry C, Sparrows Point Balto., Co., Md.	96	103				186	186 Cant get information	
16304.	MERRYMAN, George 203 East E. St.	98	105	Private	D	7 Md. Inf.	Aug. 14 1862	1864	1 5 0
16305.	LOUDEN, William 215 East E. St.	104	111	Corp.	G	205 Pa. Inf.	Sept. 2 1864	1866	1 5 0
16306.	GOODYEAR, Frederick 229 East E. St.	107	114	Sergt.	A	158 Pa. Inf.	1862	1862	1 0 0
16307.	LOFTUS, James 206 East E. St.	111	118	Corporal	K	Coles Md. Cav.	1864	1865	1 0 0
16308.	MAULFAIR, Amos C. 220 East E. St.	120	127	Corp Priv.	K	102 Pa. Inf. 48 Pa. Inf.	1864 1862	1865 1864	
16309.	WEBER, George 218 East E. St.	121	128	Priv.	C	15 Pa. Inf.	May 1861	Aug. 1864	
16310.	WIDDLE, John 216 East E. St.	122	129				186	186 Cant get no information	
16311.	SHEPLER, George 210 East E. St.	125	132				186	186 Cant get no information	
16312.	HOLLEY, Elan L. 208 East E. St.	126	133	Private	C	107 Pa. Inf.	Mar. 4 1863	June 21 1865	
16313.	McLAIN, Thomas 206 East E. St.	127	134	Priv.	I	87 Pa. Inf.	Aug. 27 1867	Nov. 12 1865	
16314.	MONTGOMERY, Thomas 202 East E. St.	129	136	Priv.	E	1st Md. Cav.	Nov. 1861	Sept. 1862	
16315.	SNYDER, Labos 208 East F. St.	136	143	Priv.	C	87 Pa. Inf.	Oct. 1861	Oct. 1864	

Special Schedule. Surviving Soldiers, Sailors, and Marines, and Widows, etc.

Page 3 S. D.: 1 ; E. D.: 456-a ; Minor Civil Division.: Maryland

1	2	3	4	5	6	7	8	9

									Yrs Mos Dys
16316.	JONES, Louis C. No. 20. Cor. D. & 4 St.	150	157			188 Pa. Inf		186	186 Could get no information
16317.	DILTY, William H. Chesapeake Mills	158	165					186	186 Could get no information
16318.	HINKLE, Chesapeake Mills	160	167					186	186 Could get no information
16319.	DeWATT, Lyman Chesapeake Mills	160	167					186	186 Could get no information
16320.	PENDERGAST, James 102 Campbelltown County	179	186	Priv.		Ordnance		1860	1864 Could get no information
16321.	WILSON, alias LEE, Willis 36 Furnace Shanty	239	246	Sailor		Aroostook	June	1862	1865
16322.	MARSHALL, John 39 Furnace Shanty	242	249	Sailor				186	186 Could get no information
16323.	LIGHT, Henry 41 Furnace Shanty	244	251	Priv.	C	4 Md. Inf.		1861	1865
16324.	GIBSON, Howell 42 Furnace Shanty	245	252	Priv.	C	32 Pa. Inf.		1864	1865
16325.	FOSTIE, Louis 50 Furnace Shanty	253	260	Priv.	C	6 U. S. C. T.		1863	1865
16326.	FLYNN, Patrick Plummer's Boarding House	265	272	Priv.	B	5 U. S. Inf.		1861	1865
16327.	CALLAHAN, John Plummer's Boarding House	265	272	Priv.				186	186 Could get no information
16328.	TAYLOR, Thomas 131 Dunn's Shanty	349	356	Priv.	B	Purnell Leg. Dept.		1861	1864
16329.	DORSEY, John 132 Dunn's Shanty	350	357	Marine	A	Colorado		1861	1865

Page No. 1
Supervisor's District No. 1
Enumeration District No. 458

Eleventh Census of the United States

SPECIAL SCHEDULE

SURVIVING SOLDIERS, SAILORS, AND MARINES, AND WIDOWS, ETC.

Persons who served in the Army, Navy, and Marine Corps of the United States during the war of the rebellion (who are survivors), and widows of such persons, in Mount Winas P. O. , County of Baltimore.
State of Maryland. enumerated in July 1890

Geo. M. Ruhl
Enumerator

1	2	3	4	5	6	7	8	9

									Yrs	Mos	Dys
16330.	CHRISTENER, Wm. A. Mount Winans	17	17 Weldon R. R. front of Petersburg, Va.	Private	B	2nd Md. Reg.	18 June 1861	3 Mar. 1865	4		
16331.	DUVALL, Edmond B. Mount Winans	27	27 Not hurt	Private	B	1st Md. Reg.	19 April 1861	19 July 1861	0	3	0
16332.	MICHAELS, Henry C. Mount Winans	11	11 Not hurt	Private	C	2nd Md. Reg.	16 March 1861	known 1865	4	0	0
16333.	CRUMP, John L. Mount Winans	18	18 Not hurt			Navy name of vessel unknown	unknown 186	unknown 186 unknown Forgotten name of Navy boat			
16334.	ORRELL, Edward B. Mt. Winans	90	19 Not hurt	Private	G	Brigade 13th Md. Home	14 Feb. 1865	29 May 1865	0	5	0
16335.	KELLY, James Mt. Winans	93	20 Not hurt	Private	C D	11 Reg. Vols. 2 Md. Vol. Battalion	15 June 1865 18 Aug. 1863	1865 6 Feb. 1864	1	0	0
16336.	EMMERICK, Ludwig Mt. Winans	95	Not hurt	Private	B	5 Md. Reg.	24 Sept. 1861	7 Sept. 1865	4		
16337.	KESTLER, Chas. J. Mt. Winans	53	Not hurt	Private		unknown	unknown 186	unknown 186 unknown Husband was absent & wife did not know			
16338.	EDWARDS, Jarret Mt. Winans	73	Not hurt	Private		unknown	unknown 186	unknown 186 unknown Husband was absent & wife did not know			
16339.	SUTTON, Gabriel Mt. Winans	74	Not hurt	Private	K	30th Col. Regt.	15 March 1864	10 December 1865	1		
16340.	DYSON, Wm. H. Mt. Winans	75	Hurt in right finger	Private		unknown	unknown 186	unknown 186 Husband was absent and wife did not know			
16341.	COOKSEY, Wm. Mt. Winans	798	Not hurt		D	Regiment 7th Georgia	May 8 1861	1862	18		

Special Schedule. Surviving Soldiers, Sailors, and Marines, and Widows, etc.

Page 2   S. D.: 1 ; E. D.: 458 ; Minor Civil Division.:

	1	2	3	4	5	6	7	8	9		
									Yrs	Mos	Dys
16342.	MUHL, Conrad Mt. Winans	201	Not hurt	Private		2nd Michgan 3rd Md.	18 May 1861	not known 186	19		
16343.	WINGATE, Ambrose Mt. Winans	210	Not hurt			Refuse to answer any questions	186	186 Refuse to answer			

16344.	KIRBY, James D. Mt. Winans	216 Not hurt			Hardy Blues of Va.	19 April 1861	6 Oct. 1863	
16345.	WELCH, Benjamin Mt. Winans	232 Not hurt	Private	D	19th Reg. Inf.	19 April 1864	1865 1 11	
16346.	GRIPP, Samuel Mt. Winans	233 Not hurt	Private		4th Wisconsin	Febry 15 1863	18 August 1866 3	
16347.	DAVIS, John John Davis Mount Winans	234			unknown	unknown 186	unknown 186 Absent from home and party did not know	
16348.	KREAMER, Christopher Mount Winans	239 237 Not hurt	Private	B	1st Maryland	May 1861	May 1866 5	
16349.	WARE, Joseph Mount Winans	241 Not hurt	Private		Winona	March 1864	March 1865 1 Wife did not know length of time in service	
16350.	SHORT, Wm. H. Mount Winans	250 Not hurt	Corporal	K	Regiment 28 Marland	unknown 186	unknown 186	unknown
16351.	ARNOLD, Wm. H. Mount Winans	253 Not hurt	Private	C	9th Maryland	May 1863	May 1865 2 Absent and wife only that he was in U. S. Army	
16352.	TAYLOR, Richard Mount Winans	244	unknown to his wife			186	186	
16353.	HALL, Charles W. Mount Winnas	282 282	Private	L	1st Ohio Heavy Artillery Dcraws 21	1863	July 25 1865	
16354.	JACKSON, Andrew Mount Winnas	U. S. A. 224	unknown		unknown	unknown 186	unknown 186	
16355.	MAHONEY, John Mount Winnas	265	unknown to his mother but draws a pension			186	186	

Special Schedule. Surviving Soldiers, Sailors, and Marines, and Widows, etc.

S. D.: 1 ; E. D.: 458 ; Minor Civil Division.: Page 3

1	2	3	4	5	6	7	8	9
								Yrs Mos Dys
16356. BROWN, Louis Mount Winans	277	277	Private	E	31st Maryland	6 May 1863	Jany 1864	18
16357. MORLELER, Geo. H. Mount Winnas	280	280	Priv.	H	10th Calvary of Va.	4 July 1862	July 1865	3
16358. WILLIAMS, Andrew Mount Winans	286	286	not known by his wife			186	186	

No.	Name / Residence			Rank	Co.	Regiment	Enlisted	Discharged	Length of Service
16359.	BLAYBURN, Wm. Mount Winans	274						186	186
16360.	√BLAYBURN, Wm. Mount Winans			Private	B	Essex County Sharp Shooter 1863		unkn 186	
16361.	MORGAN, John T. Mount Winans	295	295	not known by his daughter				186	186
16362.	MILLER, Walter B. Mount Winans	301	301	Private	G	13th Md.	not known 186	not known 186	not known
16363.	BROWN, Sam. Mount Winans	336	336	Private	D	37th Md.	Nov. 1863	March 1865	2
16364.	GREEN, John Mount Winans	266	266	Private	A	7th Md.	14 Sep. 1863	Sep. 1865	2
16365.	BUTLER, Wm. H. Mount Winans	335	335	Private	G	7 Md.	14 Nov. 1864	Nov. 1866	2
16366.	FORSTER, Henry Mount Winans	325	325	unknown to his wife				186	186
16367.	REILEY, Reuben Mount Winans	350						186	186
16368.	WILLIAMS, Resin Mount Winans	375		unknown to his wife he being absent				186	186

Special Schedule. Surviving Soldiers, Sailors, and Marines, and Widows, etc.

Page 42   S. D.: 1 ; E. D.: 458   ; Minor Civil Division.:

	1	2	3	4	5	6	7	8	9
									Yrs Mos Dys
16369.	*MICHAELS, John Mount Winans, Maryland	16	16	Private			186	186	
16370.	*HEDGEMAN, Albert Hallsville, Maryland	223	223	Sailor			186	186	

Note:-The provision of the act of March 1, 1889, under which this special enumeration of survivors of the war of the rebelloin is made, reads as follows:

That said Superintendent shall under the authority of the Secretary of the Interior, cause to be taken on a special schedule of inquiry, according to such form as he may prescribe, the names, organizations, and length of service of those who had served in the Army, Navy, or Marines Corps of the United States in the war of the rebellion, and who are survivors at the time of said inquiry, and the widows of soldiers, sailors, or marines.

The entries concerning each survivor or widow should be carefully and accurately made, so thaa\t the printed reports may contain only thoroughly trustworthy information.

Spaces are provided on this special schedule for the entry of fifty names, or more properly, term of service. The spaces are numbered consecutively from 1 to 50, and cover the four pages comprised in each schedule. The inquiries made concerning each survivor or widow call for the repetition of the number of the house and family as returned on the general population schedule (No. 1), the name, rank company, regiment or vessel, date of enlistment, date of discharge, and length of service (in years, months, and days) on the upper half of each page, and the post-office address, disability incurred, and general remarks on the lower half of each page. The column headed "Remarks" is intended to be used to cover any points not included in the forgoing inquires, and which are necessary to a complete statement of a person's term of service in any one organization.

In the case of persons having served in more than one organization, use as many spaces as may be necessary to cover their various terms of service. In the case of widows of deceased soldiers, sailors, or marines, make the entry of her name on the dotted lines, as follows: Mary J., widow of filling out the record of his service during the war, and giving under "post-office address" the Present address of his widow.   BROWN, James H.

Page No. 5 Sched - 1
Supervisor's District No. 1
Enumeration District No. 458 Special

Eleventh Census of the United States

SPECIAL SCHEDULE
SURVIVING SOLDIERS, SAILORS, AND MARINES, AND WIDOWS, ETC.

Persons who served in the Army, Navy, and Marine Corps of the United States during the war of the rebellion (who are survivors), and widows of such persons, in   St. Mary's Industrial School   , County of   Baltimore.
State of   Maryland.   enumerated in July 1890

Bro. Dominic
Enumerator

	1	2	3	4	5	6	7	8	9 Yrs Mos Dys
16371.	HOWE, William Carroll Station, Maryland	None		Priv.	A	11 Inftry U. S. A.	July 13 1863	July 13 1868	5 0 0
16372.	√HOWE, William Carroll Station, Md.	None		Priv.	C	221 Inf.	Nov. 27 1868	Nov. 27 1871	3 0 0
16373.	√HOWE, William Carroll Station, Md.	None		Priv.	A	9 Inft.	Aug. 27 1868	Aug. 27 1873 Was discharged from 29th U. S. I. was discharged at expn. services. Was discharged at expn services, age of William Howe is now 53 years. N. B. The above is taken from the Government discharges and documents which will correspond with the register of the War Department and which documents William Howe now hold.	5 0 0

Page No. 1
Supervisor's District No. 1
Enumeration District No. 459

Eleventh Census of the United States

SPECIAL SCHEDULE
SURVIVING SOLDIERS, SAILORS, AND MARINES, AND WIDOWS, ETC.

Persons who served in the Army, Navy, and Marine Corps of the United States during the war of the rebellion (who are survivors), and widows of such persons, in   2nd Pr. 13 E. District   , County of   Balto.
State of   Maryland.   enumerated in July 1890

Nelson M. Williams
Enumerator

	1	2	3	4	5	6	7	8	9 Yrs Mos Dys
16374.	Louisa Newton, widow of ROBINSON, Chas. F. St. Dennis Balto., Co., Md.	1	2				186	186	
16375.	GROSS, Ernest St. Dennis Balto., Co., Md.	14	16	Private	B	9 Md. Inf. Prisoner at Belle Island 6 mos.	24 Oct. 1863	26 Nov. 1866	3 1 2

Page -94-

16376.	SHUTLER, William H. St. Dennis Balto., Co., Md.	21	27	Private	H	1 Md. Inf.	1861	1865	3	4	
16377.	SHUTLER, Charles St. Dennis Balto., Co., Md.	21	27	Private	H	9 Md. Inf.	1865	1865		2	
16378.	OWINGS, Samuel St. Dennis Balto., Co., Md.	23	29	Private	C	3 Md. Inf.	18 July 1863	6 Feb. 1864		6	18
16379.	YOUNG, James St. Dennis Balto., Co., Md.	28	36	Corporal	C	2 Md. Cav.	24 Jan. 1863	6 Feb. 1864		7	12
16380.	Mary B., widow of McDANIEL, James St. Dennis Balto., Co., Md.	31	41				186	186			
16381.	SMALL, Levi H. (Conf) St. Dennis Balto., Co., Md.			Major	I	3 Va. Cav.	1861	1865	4		
16382.	Martha A. Williams, widow of WILLIAMS, Alexander St. Dennis Balto., Co., Md.	80	91	Orderly		2 Md. Cav.	12 Mar. 1865	close of the war 1865	1		
16383.	GANELL, William H. St. Dennis Balto., Co., Md.	81	92	Coporal	K	29 Md. Inf.	186	186			
16384.	CLEANER, Daniel St. Dennis Balto., Co., Md.	95	106	Private Rhumatism at Petersburg		2 Md. Inf.	10 Aug. 1864	20 July 1865		11	10
16385.	Emma A. Williams, widow of WILLIAMS, Chas. H. Arbutus P. O. Balto., Co., Md.	100	111	Private	H	39 Md. Inf.	26 Mar. 1864	4 Dec. 1865	1	8	19

Special Schedule. Surviving Soldiers, Sailors, and Marines, and Widows, etc.

Page

2   S. D.: 1 ; E. D.: 459   ; Minor Civil Division.: 2nd Pr. 13 E. Dist., Balto., Co., Md.

	1	2	3	4	5	6	7	8	9		
									Yrs	Mos	Dys
16386.	PREECE, Richard W. Balto., City College	150	163	Private	D	3 Md. Inf.	12 April 1865	31 July 1865		3	19
16387.	WEDDLE, William J. Carrol P. O. Balto., Co., Md.	152	165	Private C Prisoner at Florence S. C. 4 mos Prisoner at Andersonville 7 mos.		1 Md. Cav.	29 Oct. 1862	28 June 1865	2	7	29
16388.	HAMIL, Andrew T. St. Dennis P. O. Balto., Co., Md.	157	170	Private F Prisoner at Spottsylvana Court House		10 N. J. Inf.	1 Jan. 1864	1 July 1865 Re-enlisted veteran	1	6	
16389.	Sally E. Williams, wife of WILLIAMS, S. Frank St. Dennis P. O. Balto., Co., Md.	157	170				186	186			
16390.	SCOTT, William J. Arbutus P. O. Balto., Co., Md.	175	189	Private	E	Md. Cav.	20 Mar. 1864	12 Feb. 1865		10	22

16391.	BOYD, Joseph C.	191	206	Private	H	3 Md. Cav.	2 Sept. 1863	Oct. 1865	2	1	
	Carrol P. O. Balto., Co., Md.									
16392.	Margaret A. Burrows, widow of BURROWS, Hillan	198	213	Private Contracted chronic dia.	F	5 Md. Inf.	23 Oct. 1861	22 Oct. 1864	2	11	29
	Mt. Winans P. O. Balto., Co., Md.									
16393.	DAGEN, Frederick W.	216	232	Seaman		Tuscarlora	April 1865	1868 Reinlisted veteran	3		
	Mt. Winans P. O. Balto., Co., Md.									
16394.	WARRER, John N.	227	244	Private Was slightly bruised on left knee with a piece of shell	E	3 Md. Inf.	12 Nov. 1861	12 Nov. 1864	3		
	Mt. Winans P. O. Balto., Co., Md.									
16395.	Maggie Kakafer, widow of KAKAFER, August	229	246	Private Shot in left wrist	F	1 Md. Cav.	1861	1865	4		
	Arbutus P. O. Balto., Co., Md.									
16396.	Mary V., widow of NEBER,	241	271				186	186			
	Carroll P. O. Balto., Co., Md.									
16397.	COLLINS, William H.	258	282	Private Gun shot in right arm	E	39 Md. Inf.	26 Mar. 1864	4 Dec. 1865	1	8	8
	Arbutus P. O. Balto., Co., Md.									
16398.	CROWNER, James	143	156	Private			186	186			
16399.	ROSS, Thomas	65	76				186	186			
	Relay 13 E. Dist. Balto., Co., Md.									

Page No.
Supervisor's District No. 1
Enumeration District No. 460

Eleventh Census of the United States

SPECIAL SCHEDULE

SURVIVING SOLDIERS, SAILORS, AND MARINES, AND WIDOWS, ETC.

Persons who served in the Army, Navy, and Marine Corps of the United States during the war of the rebellion (who are survivors), and widows of such persons, in   Bay View Asylum   , County of   Baltimore   ,
State of   Maryland.   enumerated in July 1890

Wm. H. Cole
Enumerator

1	2	3	4	5	6	7	8	9
								Yrs Mos Dys
16400. *ZWINK, John F. Bay View Asylum			Sol.			186	186	
16401. *RILEY, Thomas Bay View Asylum			Sailor			186	186	
16402. *COLEMAN, George W. Bay View Asylum			Sailor			186	186	

No.	Name	Rank	Col A	Col B
16403.	*FLYNN, Edward Bay View Asylum	Soldier	186	186
16404.	*McFEE, Robert Bay View Asylum	Soldier	186	186
16405.	*ARMACOST, William H. Bay View Asylum	Soldier	186	186
16406.	*McKENZIE, David Bay View Asylum	Soldier	186	186
16407.	*BAARS, August Bay View Asylum	Soldier	186	186
16408.	*FREEBURGER, Columbus M. Bay View Asylum	Soldier	186	186
16409.	*MILBURN, Thomas H. Bay View Asylum	Soldier	186	186
16410.	*WHITE, Michael H. Bay View Asylum	Soldier	186	186
16411.	*KESTER, Jacob Bay View Asylum	Soldier	186	186

Special Schedule. Surviving Soldiers, Sailors, and Marines, and Widows, etc.

Page

S. D.:   ; E. D.:   ; Minor Civil Division.:

	1	2	3	4	5	6	7	8	9
									Yrs Mos Dys
16412. *BURNS, William A. Bay View Asylum				Sol.				186	186
16413. *NORRIS, James H. Bay View Asylum				Sailor				186	186
16414. *MAKEL, Philips Bay View Asylum				Sol.				186	186
16415. *DORSEY, James Bay View Asylum				Sailor				186	186
16416. *FOUNTAIN, Stephen Bay View Asylum				Sol.				186	186
16417. *THOMAS George Bay View Asylum				Sol.				186	186
16418. *COX, Allen Bay View Asylum				Sol.				186	186
16419. *THOMPSON, Joseph F. Bay View Asylum				Sol.				186	186

	1	2	3	4	5	6	7	8	9
16420.	*KNEUCKER, John Bay View Asylum			Sol.			186	186	
16421.	*ASHLAND, James Bay View Asylum			Sol.			186	186	
16422.	*DUNCAN, John F. Bay View Asylum			Sol.			186	186	
16423.	*SHAW, William K. Bay View Asylum			Sol.			186	186	
16424.	*HIGHLAND, George W. Bay View Asylum			Sol.			186	186	
16425.	*BAKER, Catharine J. Bay View Asylum			widow of U. S. Soldier			186	186	

Special Schedule. Surviving Soldiers, Sailors, and Marines, and Widows, etc.

Page

S. D.:   ; E. D.:   ; Minor Civil Division.:

	1	2	3	4	5	6	7	8	9
									Yrs Mos Dys
16426.	*BURKE, Ann widow Bay View Asylum			Soldier			186	186	
16427.	*DOWNEY, Sarah J. Bay View Asylum			Soldier			186	186	
16428.	*EDWARDS, Catherine Bay View Asylum			Soldier			186	186	
16429.	*LARKIN, Mary Bay View Asylum			Soldier			186	186	
16430.	*SPEAR, John C. Bay View Asylum			Soldier			186	186	
16431.	*SMITH, Thomas Bay View Asylum			Soldier			186	186	
16432.	*√SMITH, Thomas Bay View Asylum			Soldier			186	186	
16433.	*FOGARTY, Thomas Bay View Asylum			Marine			186	186	
16434.	*KROETZKAMP, Henry Bay View Asylum			Sol.			186	186	
16435.	*GESFORD, John Bay View Asylum			Sol.			186	186	

Page No.
Supervisor's District No. 1
Enumeration District No. 460

Eleventh Census of the United States

SPECIAL SCHEDULE
SURVIVING SOLDIERS, SAILORS, AND MARINES, AND WIDOWS, ETC.

Persons who served in the Army, Navy, and Marine Corps of the United States during the war of the rebellion (who are survivors), and widows of such persons, in Bay View Asylum , County of Baltimore ,
State of Maryland. enumerated in July 1890

Wm. H. Cole
Enumerator

	1	2	3	4	5	6	7	8	9
									Yrs Mos Dys
16436.	*HARVEY, Philip Bay View Asylum			Sol.			186	186	
16437.	*DOYLE, John Bay View Asylum			Sol.	U. S.		186	186	
16438.	*LEWIS, Adelia Bay View Asylum			Ma.	U. S.		186	186	
16439.	*WISE, Sarah Bay View Asylum			W. - Sol.	U. S.		186	186	
16440.	*BRADLEY, Martha Bay View Asylum			W. - Sol.	U. S.		186	186	
16441.	*WATSON, Robert W. Bay View Asylum			Sail	U. S.		186	186	
16442.	*GARRISON, Alexander Bay View Asylum			Sol.	U. S.		186	186	
16443.	*SMITH, Larkin H. Bay View Asylum			Sol.	U. S.		186	186	
16444.	*GROSS, Thomas Bay View Asylum			Sol.	U. S.		186	186	
16445.	*MILLER, Thomas Bay View Asylum			Sol.	U. S.		186	186	
16446.	*LYNCH, Ellen Bay View Asylum			Wid Sol.	U. S.		186	186	
16447.	*RIDENGER, John A. Bay View Asylum			Sol.	U. S.		186	186	

Special Schedule. Surviving Soldiers, Sailors, and Marines, and Widows, etc.

Page

S. D.: ; E. D.: ; Minor Civil Division.:

	1	2	3	4	5	6	7	8	9		
									Yrs	Mos	Dys
16448.	BARRY, John			Sol.	U.S.			186	186		
16449.	FURRIER, Nathan G. C.			Sol.	U.S.			186	186		
16450.	BRUNER, John L.			Sol.	U.S.			186	186		
16451.	TURFORD, John			Sol.	U.S.			186	186		
16452.	CARTER, Wm.			Sol.	U.S.			186	186		
16453.	SCHRINER, John G.			Sol.	U.S.			186	186		
16454.	BENNETT, Patrick			Sol.	U.S.			186	186		

Page No
Supervisor's District No. 1
Enumeration District No.

Eleventh Census of the United States

SPECIAL SCHEDULE
SURVIVING SOLDIERS, SAILORS, AND MARINES, AND WIDOWS, ETC.

Persons who served in the Army, Navy, and Marine Corps of the United States during the war of the rebellion (who are survivors), and widows of such persons, in , County of Baltimore ,
State of Md. enumerated in June 1890

Enumerator

	1	2	3	4	5	6	7	8	9		
									Yrs	Mos	Dys
16455.	HYDE, Edward J. 1300 E. Biddle St.	23	28 Hernia	Capt.	B	4th Md. Infty	June 28 1862	Aug. 7 1863	1	1	11
						Resignation accepted on surgeons certificate of disability					
16456.	ROSENTHAL, Julius Julius Rosenthal Balto., Md.	10	12	Private	G	15 Md. Inft.	1865	1 Sept. 1865	1	6	15
16457.	KERR, Robt. J. Robt. J. Kerr Balto., Md.	17	20	Private	G	15 Md. Inft.	30 Mar. 1865	29 May 1865		3	
16458.	HALL, William Baltimore, Md.	19	22	Private	A	59 N.Y. Inft.	22 Aug. 1862	June 1865	2	10	
16459.	LUBER, John Baltimore, Md.	24	30	Private	Band	2 Md. Inft.	7 Oct. 1861	17 Aug. 1862		10	10
16460.	Alias Jno. Heinzelman SMITH, John Baltimore, Md.	26	32	Private	B	1 Md. Cal.	Feb. 1862	Aug. 1865	3	6	

16461.	KRODER, August Baltimore, Md.		68	89	Private	D	10 Md. Inf.	8 Jan. 1863	29 June 1864	6	
16462.	WHARTON, George D. Baltimore, Md.		64	81	Private	C	1 Md. Inf.	29 Aug. 1861	13 1864	3	14
16463.	MANNIS, Emanuel Baltimore, Md.	Cecelia Mannis, w. of	68	115	Private	E	2 Md. Inf.	2 July 1861	21 June 1865	3	11
16464.	ERNST, Anton Baltimore, Md.	Regina Ernst, w. of	63	100	Private	B	2 Md. Inf.	1861	1864	3	
16465.	FADER, Chas. W. Baltimore, Md.		87	155	Sergent	K	1 Md. Inf.	19 Apl 1861	19 Apl 1863	2	
16466.	MORRIS, William E. Baltimore, Md.		105	179	Private	A	11 Md. Inf.	11 May 1864	1 Oct. 1864	4	17

Special Schedule. Surviving Soldiers, Sailors, and Marines, and Widows, etc.

Page 2   S. D.:   ; E. D.:   ; Minor Civil Division.:

1	2	3	4	5	6	7	8	9
								Yrs Mos Dys
16467. LINDIG, Ernest Elizabeth Lindig, w. of Baltimore, Md.	130	227	Corporal Private	F	3 U. S. Art.	186	1863	5

Page No.
Supervisor's District No. 1
Enumeration District No.

Eleventh Census of the United States

SPECIAL SCHEDULE
SURVIVING SOLDIERS, SAILORS, AND MARINES, AND WIDOWS, ETC.

Persons who served in the Army, Navy, and Marine Corps of the United States during the war of the rebellion (who are survivors), and widows of such persons, in   Samuel Ready Asylum   , County of   Balto., City & County   ,
State of   Md.   enumerated in June 1890

Clara H. Steiner
Enumerator

1	2	3	4	5	6	7	8	9
								Yrs Mos Dys
16468. *GREEN, Catherine - widow Asylum - cor. North & Harford Ave.						186	186	

Page No. 1   Eleventh Census of the United States

Supervisor's District No. 1st Maryland
Enumeration District No. Special

SPECIAL SCHEDULE
SURVIVING SOLDIERS, SAILORS, AND MARINES, AND WIDOWS, ETC.

Persons who served in the Army, Navy, and Marine Corps of the United States during the war of the rebellion (who are survivors), and widows of such persons, in The U. S. Marine Hospital , County of Baltimore , State of Maryland. enumerated in June 1890

Wm. H. H. Hutton, Jr.
Enumerator

	1	2	3	4	5	6	7	8	9 Yrs Mos Dys
16469.	HUTTON, William H. H. U. S. Marine Hospital Baltimore, Md.	1	1	Private Loss of hearing right ear	H	20 Ill. Vol.	June 17 1861	Aug. 28 1862 Battle of Shiloh Tenn., Apr. 7th 1862	1 2 11
16470.	√HUTTON, William H. H. U. S. Marine Hospital Baltimore, Md.	1	1	Sergeant Gun shot wound right infraclavicular region	D	104 Ill. Vol.	Sept. 2 1862	Mar. 8 1865 Battle of Missionary Ridge, Tenn. Nov. 24th 1864	2 6 6
16471.	√HUTTON, William H. H.	1	1	Steward		U. S. Army	Mar. 8 1865	Apr. 1 1871	6 0 23 9 9 10
16472.	SULLIVAN, John # 45 Market Space Baltimore, Md.	3	4	Private Partial loss hearing left ear	D	6 Cal. Vol.	Aug. 23 1864	Dec. 19 1865	1 3 26
16473.	MACK, Mathias # 53 Lawrence St. New York City	3	4	Private None	B	112 Pa. Vol.	Dec. 24 1861	Apr. 16 1862	3 22
16474.	GILLESPIE, John D. # 617 S. Front St. Philadelphia, Penna.	3	4	Private Slight flesh wound right leg		1st Maine	May 2 1862	Feb. 1864	1 8 28
16475.	√GILLESPIE, John D.	3	4	Seaman		Powhatan	Jan. 1864	1865	1 2 8 28
16476.	GOLDTHORPE, William # 227 President St. Baltimore, Md.	3	4	Private None	M	1 Art. U. S. A.	Oct. 1 1857	Oct. 1 1862	5 0 0
16477.	√GOLDTHORPE, William	3	4	Private	E	4 Art. U. S. A.	Oct. 15 1862	Oct. 15 1865	3 0 0
16478.	√GOLDTHORPE, William	3	4	Private	E	4 Art. U. S. A.	Oct. 15 1865	Oct. 15 1868	3 0 0 11 0 0

Special Schedule. Surviving Soldiers, Sailors, and Marines, and Widows, etc.

Page 2 S. D.: 1st Maryland ; E. D.: Special ; Minor Civil Division.: U. S. Marine Hospital

	1	2	3	4	5	6	7	8	9 Yrs Mos Dys
16479.	CLARK, George Tremont Hancock County, Maine	3	4	Private None	H	5 ME. Vol.	186	186	4 0 0

	1	2	3	4	5	6	7	8	9
16480.	MILLER, Thomas U. S. Marine Hospital Baltimore, Md.	3	4		Private Scalp wound from sabre	D	2 Cav. U. S. A.	Aug. 15 1861	Aug. 15 186	4 0 0

Page No. 1
Supervisor's District No. Special 73
Enumeration District No. Special

Eleventh Census of the United States

SPECIAL SCHEDULE
SURVIVING SOLDIERS, SAILORS, AND MARINES, AND WIDOWS, ETC.

Persons who served in the Army, Navy, and Marine Corps of the United States during the war of the rebellion (who are survivors), and widows of such persons, in Hebrew Hospital & Asylum , City of Baltimore ,
State of Maryland. enumerated in June 1890

M. Friedmann
Enumerator

	1	2	3	4	5	6	7	8	9 Yrs Mos Dys
16481.	HECKSCHER, Joseph N. Hebrew Hospital Balto., Md.			None	Private	H	9th N. Y.	186	186	1 6 5
16482.	Hannah Kaiser, widow of KAISER, Charles Hebrew Hospital Balto., Md.							186	186 Don't remember anything regarding it she being too old	

Supplied by E. Goldsborough

Page No.
Supervisor's District No.
Enumeration District No. Special Notre Dame

Eleventh Census of the United States

SPECIAL SCHEDULE
SURVIVING SOLDIERS, SAILORS, AND MARINES, AND WIDOWS, ETC.

Persons who served in the Army, Navy, and Marine Corps of the United States during the war of the rebellion (who are survivors), and widows of such persons, in Notre Dame , County of Balto ,
State of Maryland. enumerated in June 1890

Sister Mary Clarissa
Enumerator

	1	2	3	4	5	6	7	8	9 Yrs Mos Dys
16483.	*LINDERMAN, Margaret widow Aisquith St.							186	186	

Page No. 1
Supervisor's District No. 1
Enumeration District No. Special

Eleventh Census of the United States

SPECIAL SCHEDULE
SURVIVING SOLDIERS, SAILORS, AND MARINES, AND WIDOWS, ETC.

Persons who served in the Army, Navy, and Marine Corps of the United States during the war of the rebellion (who are survivors), and widows of such persons, in 2nd District , County of Baltimore ,
State of Maryland. enumerated in June 1890

W. Ballard Smith
Enumerator

	1	2	3	4	5	6	7	8	9 Yrs Mos Dys
16484.	WEAVER, Lewis McDonogh P. O.	6	6	Private	A	6 Md. Inf.	11 Aug. 1862	24 June 1865	2 10 13

Page No. One
Supervisor's District No. 1
Enumeration District No. Special

Eleventh Census of the United States

SPECIAL SCHEDULE
SURVIVING SOLDIERS, SAILORS, AND MARINES, AND WIDOWS, ETC.

Persons who served in the Army, Navy, and Marine Corps of the United States during the war of the rebellion (who are survivors), and widows of such persons, in Baltimore City Jails , County of Baltimore
State of Maryland. enumerated in June 1890

C. Frank Edwards
Enumerator

	1	2	3	4	5	6	7	8	9 Yrs Mos Dys
16485.	DIETZ, John N.							186	186
16486.	SNYDER, John							186	186
16487.	FRANCIS, Nicholas							186	186
16488.	MASON, Joseph							186	186
16489.	DRANE, David F.							186	186
16490.	JOHNSON, John							186	186
16491.	SANDS, Luther S.							186	186
16492.	HANNAN, Francis C.							186	186
16493.	CRONAN, Daniel							186	186
16494.	BRAWNER, Joseph							186	186
16495.	DAVIS, Joshua							186	186

16496. O'BRIAN, John							186	186	

Special Schedule. Surviving Soldiers, Sailors, and Marines, and Widows, etc.

Page 2   S. D.:   ; E. D.:   ; Minor Civil Division.:

	1	2	3	4	5	6	7	8	9
									Yrs Mos Dys
16497. BETZ, Charles R.							186	186	
16498. DITTMAN, John G.							186	186	
16499. GOSNELL, George N.							186	186	
16500. WISEMAN, James							186	186	
16501. *MITCHELL, John W. Baltimore City Jail	10						186	186	
16502. *WALES, Wm. R. Baltimore City Jail	305						186	186	

Page No. 1
Supervisor's District No. 1 Special
Enumeration District No. Maryland General Hospital

Eleventh Census of the United States

SPECIAL SCHEDULE
SURVIVING SOLDIERS, SAILORS, AND MARINES, AND WIDOWS, ETC.

Persons who served in the Army, Navy, and Marine Corps of the United States during the war of the rebellion (who are survivors), and widows of such persons, in Maryland General Hospital , City of Baltimore ,
State of Maryland. enumerated in June 1890

David Williams M. D.
Enumerator

	1	2	3	4	5	6	7	8	9
									Yrs Mos Dys
16503. BROUGHTON, Charles C. Baltimore, Maryland	1	1	Private	E	10 Colored Vol.	Dec. 1863	Nov. 1865	1 11	

Page No. 1
Supervisor's District No. 1
Enumeration District No.

Eleventh Census of the United States

SPECIAL SCHEDULE
SURVIVING SOLDIERS, SAILORS, AND MARINES, AND WIDOWS, ETC.

Persons who served in the Army, Navy, and Marine Corps of the United States during the war of the rebellion (who are survivors), and widows of such persons, in Fort McHenry, Baltimore, County of Baltimore, State of Maryland, enumerated in June 1890

Louis E. Roucharf
Enumerator

	1	2	3	4	5	6	7	8	9 Yrs Mos Dys
16504.	BOHMER, August Fort McHenry Baltimore, Md.	1	1	Pvte	F	19 Mass. Inf.	24 July 1864	29 June 1865	11 5
16505.	Loftus John, alias SMITH, Hugh B. Fort McHenry Baltimore, Md.	1	1	Pvte	A	1 Jersey Vol.	10 Apl 1861	10 July 1861	3
16506.	LESCHINGER, Felix Fort McHenry Baltimore, Md.	1	1	Pvte	K	3 Wis. Cav.	25 Aug. 1862	25 Aug. 1865	3
16507.	WARREN, John M. Fort McHenry Baltimore, Md.	1	1	Pvte		Louisiana Guard Artillery, New Orleans	26 Apl. 1861	186 Paroled April 9, 1865	
16508.	BOWER, Alfred B. Fort McHenry Baltimore, Md.	1	1	1 Lt.		28 Ala. Inf.	11 Mch 1862	186 Paroled May 1865	
16509.	BERNER, Richard Fort McHenry Baltimore, Md.	1	1	Pvte	D	Clareck 35 Zouaves	10 Mch 1865	10 July 1865 Mustered out	4
16510.	KNOWER, Edward C. Fort McHenry Baltimore, Md.	2	2	Capt.	I	4 N. Y. Art.	3 Feby 1862	31 Dec. 1866 Mustered out	4 10 28
16511.	HAROLD, Christopher W. Fort McHenry Baltimore, Md.	4	4	1 Lt.	B	1 N. H. Art.	7 Nov. 1862	11 Sept. 1865 Mustered out	2 10 4
16512.	HAUPT, William Fort McHenry Baltimore, Md.	8	8	Pvte	H	34 U. S. Inf.	1 Sept. 1864	1 Sept. 1867	3
16513.	THURSTON, George A. Fort McHenry Baltimore, Md.	9	9	Capt.		1 Md. Inf.	10 Apr. 1864	15 Dec. 1865 Mustered out	1 8 5
16514.	LIVINGSTON, LaRhett L. Fort McHenry Baltimore, Md.	14	14	Capt.		3 U. S. Art.	26 Oct. 1861	remained 186 in service	
16515.	BURNS, Joseph Fort McHenry Baltimore, Md.	14	14	Pvte	K	5 Pa. Cav.	19 Aug. 1861	19 Aug. 1864	3

All in U. S. Army now

Special Schedule. Surviving Soldiers, Sailors, and Marines, and Widows, etc.

Page 2   S. D.: 1   ; E. D.:   ; Minor Civil Division.:

										Yrs	Mos	Dys
16516.	SELMER, Charles Fort McHenry Baltimore, Md.	19	19	Capt.		11 Me. Inf.	13 June 1863	9 Feby 1866		2	7	27
16517.	MYRICK, John R. Fort McHenry Baltimore, Md.	20	20	Lieut.	B	13 N. Y. 3 U. S. Art.	23 Apr. 1861	Remained in service 186				

Added by A. M. Sliddord Tr. Clerk Oct. 30 - 1890

Page No. 1
Supervisor's District No. 1
Enumeration District No. Md. Gen. Hospital

Eleventh Census of the United States

SPECIAL SCHEDULE
SURVIVING SOLDIERS, SAILORS, AND MARINES, AND WIDOWS, ETC.

Persons who served in the Army, Navy, and Marine Corps of the United States during the war of the rebellion (who are survivors), and widows of such persons, in   Md. Gen. Hospital   ,   County of   Baltimore   ,
State of   Maryland.   enumerated in June 1890

David Williams M. D.
Enumerator

1	2	3	4	5	6	7	8	9
								Yrs Mos Dys
16518. BROUGHTON, Charles C. Linden Ave. Baltimore	1	1	Sol.				186	186

Page No.
Supervisor's District No.
Enumeration District No. Special - Maryland Penitentiary

Eleventh Census of the United States

SPECIAL SCHEDULE
SURVIVING SOLDIERS, SAILORS, AND MARINES, AND WIDOWS, ETC.

Persons who served in the Army, Navy, and Marine Corps of the United States during the war of the rebellion (who are survivors), and widows of such persons, in   Baltimore   ,   County of   Baltimore   ,
State of   Maryland.   enumerated in June 1890

Maryland Penitentiary

Louis G. Zinkhan
Enumerator

1	2	3	4	5	6	7	8	9
								Yrs Mos Dys
16519. BROOKS, John Maryland P.			Private Shot in left arm	A	6 Penn. Inf.	May 1862	April 1865	2 11
16520. WORTHINGTON, Joseph Maryland P.			Private Shot in face, right ankle & leg & side	I	1 Md. Inf	nearly 1864	1865	1 year
16521. ROBERT, Henry Maryland P.			Orderly Sergeant Shot in right leg		33 N. C. A.	186	186	2 6

16522.	Edward Turner alias WILLIAMS, Frank Maryland P.		Private	F	7 Md. Inf.	Sept. 1863	1866	3	6
16523.	KNOWLING, John Henry Maryland P.		Private	F	98 N. Y. Inf.	Oct. 1864 Not regulary enlisted	Aug. 1865		9
16524.	Henry Braun alias LENDAN, Henry Maryland P.	Lost left eye by cap. & 2nd finger right hand	Private	B	Pa. Inf.	1864	1866	1	6
16525.	SUPPLE, James Maryland P.		1st Class Boy		U. S. Steamer Mercury	May 23 1864	1866	1	7
16526.	JACKSON, Jonas Maryland P.	Ruptured	Powder Boy		Gun boat Astrilla	May 1863	1864		9
16527.	SPURRIER, Edward Maryland P.	Rheumatism & heart disease	Corporal	F	8 Md. Inf.	Aug. 18 1862 Discharged on Surgeon's certificate	Jan. 13 1863	4	25
16528.	KEEPERS, Jr. Joseph Maryland P.	Chronic diarrhea	Private	C	26 Penn. Inf.	March 11 1863 Home on furlough & released by reason of disability by the captain	186	1	6
16529.	DUNCAN, Charles Mason Maryland P.	Spine injured by kick of mule gun shot wound in right knee	Private 2nd Lieut.	N H	14 Conn. 39 N. Y. Inf.	Aug. 23 1863 Promoted from Comp. H - 14th Conn. to 39th N. Y.	July 6 1865	1 11	13
16530.	THOMPSON, William Maryland P.		Private	I	17 Penn. Cav.	1864	1865		10

Special Schedule. Surviving Soldiers, Sailors, and Marines, and Widows, etc.

Page 2   S. D.: 1   ; E. D.:   ; Minor Civil Division.:

1	2	3	4	5	6	7	8	9
								Yrs Mos Dys
16531. PEAKER, William H. Maryland P.	Rheumatism		Private	S	30 Md. Inf.	Mch 15 1864 Transferred from the Army to the Navy	June 1864	3
16532. √PEAKER, William H. Maryland P.			Coal Passer		Mt. Vernon to Vanderville	June 1864	1867	3
16533. Jacob Freeland, alias FRISBY, Jacob Maryland P.	Injured in head by shell shot		Private	D	2 U. S. Inf.	1864	Feby 1866	3
16534. BROWN, Moses Maryland P.			Private		U. S. Inf.	May 186 Went home on furlough, got sick & didn't return	Dec. 186	7 8

#	1	2	3	4	5	6	7	8	9
16535.	GOVER, Alfred Maryland P.			Private Shot in the head	A	13 Md. inf.	Feby 1865	June 29 1865 Re-enlisted in regular U. S. Army	4
16536.	Charles Williams, alias MOORE, Richard J. Maryland P.			Private	D	23 U. S. Inf.	1863	1864 Transferred from the Army to Navy	1 6
16537.	Charles Williams, alias √MOORE, Richard J. Maryland P.			Transferred from Army to Navy Landsman		Tuscarora	Navy 1864	1865	9
16538.	SEAS, Sanford E. Maryland P.			Private Ankle strained, rheumatism	B	1 Penn. Art.	Feby 19 1864	June 1865	1 3
16539.	LAVERN, William E. Maryland P.			Private Spine injured by timber falling whilst on guard at Point Lookout, Md.	H	5 Mass. Vol. Cal.	1863	1865	1 10
16540.	CARROLL, Abraham (Conf) Maryland P.			Private Diarrhea & kidney trouble	C	39 Md. Inf.	1864	Dec. 1865	1
16541.	COTTMAN, Nathan Maryland P.			Private Shot in hand (thumb off)	I	9 Md. Inf.	Nov. 1863	1866	3
16542.	Nicholas Harden, alias HORSEY, Howard Maryland P.			Private Shot in left leg	A	May or 1st Dist. Col. Inf.	1863	June 1865	2
16543.	BUCK, Solomon S. Maryland P.			2nd Lieut. Typhoid fever	E	about 208 Penn. Vol. Inf.	Sept. 1 1864	June 1865	9
16544.	HUGHES, Edward Maryland P.			Private Shot through right arm Aug. 19th '64	D	61 Va. Inf.	1861	1864	3 6

Special Schedule. Surviving Soldiers, Sailors, and Marines, and Widows, etc.

Page

S. D.:   ; E. D.:   ; Minor Civil Division.:

#	1	2	3	4	5	6	7	8	9
									Yrs Mos Dys
16545.	DAVIS, Joseph Maryland Penitentiary			Sergeant Bullet wound through left shoulder & loss of 2nd finger of left hand	B	7th Louisiana Inf.	July 14 1863	May 14 1864	10
16546.	√DAVIS, Joseph Maryland Penitentiary			Cabin boy None		Frigate Potomac	June 1861	April 1863	10
16547.	WHITESEL, Charles Maryland Penitentiary			Corporal None	K	45 Penn. Inf.	July 2 1863	Oct. 1863	3
16548.	JONES, Isaace Maryland Penitentiary			Private None	F	2 U. S. Inf.	Sept. 1863	Nov. 1865	2 2

16549.	SHAW, John A. Maryland Penitentiary		Private Rheumatism & rupture & hearing	E	Inf. 155 Penn. Zouaves	Aug. 22 1862	June 5 1865	2	9	18
16550.	CARROLL, William Maryland Penitentiary	None	Landsman		Oneida	May 27 1864	Aug. 9 1865	1	2	13
16551.	*KEENAN, Isaac Maryland Penitentiary	10				186	186			
16552.	*WEST, Frank Maryland Penitentiary	21	Sailor			186	186			
16553.	*STANTON, John Maryland Penitentiary	146	Sailor			186	186			

Page No.
Supervisor's District No. 1
Enumeration District No. St. J.

Eleventh Census of the United States

SPECIAL SCHEDULE
SURVIVING SOLDIERS, SAILORS, AND MARINES, AND WIDOWS, ETC.

Persons who served in the Army, Navy, and Marine Corps of the United States during the war of the rebellion (who are survivors), and widows of such persons, in St. Joseph's Hospital , City of Baltimore
State of Maryland. enumerated in June 1890

Shelden G. Evans M. D.
Enumerator

	1	2	3	4	5	6	7	8	9
									Yrs Mos Dys
16554.	Teresa, widow of HIMMER, Charles St. Joseph's Hospital Balto., Md.			Private	B	1 Md. Cav. Husband accused of deserting very inadequate facts	Sep. 1861	Sep. 1862	1
16555.	Elizabeth Wohlfast, widow of WOHLFAST, John St. Joseph's Hospital			Private		Knows nothing of husband		186	186
16556.	Caroline Harvey, widow of HARVEY, Harrison St. Joseph's Hospital		Shot in arm	Private	1	2 Md. Inf.		186	186
16557.	CODY, John St. Joseph's Hospital		None incurred	Sailor			Sep. 1861	186	

INDEX

ABBOTT, Charles C. 16269.
ABNER, James J. 15538.
ADAMS, Jacob 15786, Samuel 15568,
AGNUS, Felix 15454.
AHLEE, John 16195.
AILER, Peter 15378.
AKEHURST, Charles 15965, David 16017.
ALBAUGH, Charles 16026,
ALDER, John R. 15541.
ALLEN, Christopher 15990, Solomon C. 16066.
AMBROSE, Geo. W. 15526, Joshua 15794.
ANDERSON, B. F. 15634, Susan E. 15634.
ANDREWS, Sarah E. 15642, Wm. 15642.
ANDSON, Steven J. 15435.
APPLEBY, Raisin 15972,
ARCHABALD, James 15818.
ARMACOST, Melchior 15847, William H. 16405.
ARMSTRONG, Solomon 15835.
ARNOLD, Wm. H. 16351.
ASHER, James H. 16182.
ASHLAND, James 16421.
AULT, Conrad 15336.
AUSTIN, Ferdinand 15517.
AYERS, Henry 16034.
BAARS, August 16407.
BADER, John 16219.
BAHN, John C. 15570.
BAILEY, Caleb 15933, Frederick A. 15720, John D. 15281.
BAKER, Catharine J. 16425, Henry F. 15701, Isaac C. 15659, John 15529.
BALELKE, Fred. W. 16116.
BALL, Eli S. 15702, T. Savell 15430,
BANBERGER, William W. 15405.
BANBLITZ, Daniel 15608.
BARNES, George W. 16285, Uriah 15393,
BARTEN, Isaac I. 16044.
BARTHOLOME, Christian 15380.
BATTLE, George 15507.
BAUBLITZ, Cornelius 15848, George 15731, John 15605, Margaret 15605, Samuel 15616.
BAUGHMAN, Joshua 15977, Mary F. 15977.
BAYNE, William 15893.
BEAVER, Oliver 15511.
BECKERD, Frederick J. 16220.
BEDFORD, William D. 15937.
BELL, James 15544, Joshua 15429, Nelson 16076, Phillip 16049, William 15961.
BELT, Benjamin F. 15560.
BENNETT, Patrick 16454.
BENTON, Francis 16070.

BERNER, Richard 16509.
BERRY, George 15781, Richard A. 15288.
BESS, Benjamin 15931.
BETZ, Charles R. 16497, John 15870.
BEWLEY, Isaac T. 15253,
BIRD, Caleb 15933.
BISHOP, Ansinette 15425, George W. John L. 15316, Thomas 15425.
BLAKENEY, Sarah 16109.
BLAYBURN, Wm. 16359, 16360.
BLIZZARD, John A. 15525.
BLUCHER, Albert 15996.
BOEDERSON, Orlando 15273.
BOHMER, August 16504.
BOLLINGER, George 15627.
BOLTE, Henry 15502.
BOND, Geo. W. 16069, James D. 15677, William 16262.
BOOTMAN, John W. 16161.
BORTLE, John E. 15371.
BOSLEY, John H. 15558, Levi 15516, William H. 15559.
BOSTICK, William Henry 16096.
BOWEN, Frank 16106,
BOWERS, Alfred B. 16508, Andrew F. 15522, Barnhard 16054.
BOYD, Joseph C. 16391.
BOYLE, Thomas B. 15459.
BRADLEY, Martha 16440.
BRADRY, Nathan 16030.
BRADY, James 15241, James W. 15262.
BRAINARD, Edgar J. 15861.
BRATT, James E. 16245, Samuel J. 16270.
BRAUN, Henry 16524.
BRAWNER, Joseph 16494.
BRECKENRIDGE, Robert 15461.
BRENBERGER, John E. 15465.
BRENEMAN, Christian 16296.
BRENIZE, Joseph K. 15411.
BRICKNER, John 15892, Lena 15892.
BRIHEIM, August 15528.
BRILL, Henry 15265.
BROOKS, Albert 15816, Albert A. 15905, John 16519.
BROUGHTON, Charles C. 16503, 16518.
BROWN, Aaron 15960, Chas. H. 15457, David 15935, Enoch 15388, Ezra F. 15926, George W. 15317, Jacob F. H. 15531, Louis 16356, Magnus 16147, Moses 16534, Nancy 15457, Richard A. 15268, Robert M. 15444, Sam. 16363,
BRUMMEL, David O. 15499, Joseph 15477.
BRUNER, John L. 16450.
BRYDON, John H. 12164.

BRYSON, Ferdmand R. 16163.
BUCHANAN, Nathan 15762.
BUCHANNAN, George 15505.
BUCK, John H. 16148, Solomon 16543.
BUCKINGHAM, Harriet 15312.
BUETTNER, Edward 16149.
BULL, Christopher 15591, Joshua L. 15695.
BULLING, William H. 15857.
BUMP, Jesse E. 15643.
BUPP, Henry D. 15625.
BURGOYNE, Henry A. 15542.
BURK, John 15252.
BURKE, Ann 16426, John 15249, Nicholas 15889, Sarah J. 15889.
BURNINE, James 15912.
BURNS, John T. 15708, Joseph 16515, Richard N. 15711, William A. 16412, Wm. D. 15491.
BURRIER, Solomon 16160.
BURROWS, Hillan 16392, Margaret A. 16392.
BURRUSS, William J. 15877.
BURTON, John 15942.
BUSH, John 15646, Tammy 15646.
BUTLER, James 15963, William H. 16100, Wm. H. 16365.
BUTT, James J. 13867.
BUTTON, James O. 16268.
CALDWELL, John J. 15510.
CALLAHAN, John 16327.
CAMERON, George H. 15728, John M. 15730.
CAMPBELL, Andrew 15498, Geo. W. 15274, Harriet 15498, John G. 16093.
CAREY, Charlotte 15804, Edward W. 15804.
CARMAN, Arthur S. 15683.
CARRINGTON, Josiah 15469.
CARROLL, Abraham 16540, Charles 16072, William 16550.
CARTER, Dennis 15895, John W. 15989, Joseph M. Uriah 15894, Wm. 16452.
CARVALL, Charles 15932.
CASKEY, John F. 15666.
CASSELL, Alexander 15987.
CASSIDY, Edward S. 16105, Michael 10854.
CASTEN, Bennett 15836.
CASWELL, Charles 15676, Sarah Cole 15676.
CHALFANT, George F. 15650.
CHANDLER, William E. 16143.
CHANEY, Charles 15839, Louis 15907.
CHANY, John 15449, 15472.
CHASE, Thomas 15808.
CHENOWETH, William H. 15451.
CHENWITH, Thomas J. 15891.
CHENWORTH, John T. 16233.
CHILDS, Benjamin F. 15437, Summerfield 15351.
CHINWORTH, John H. 15504, William 15493.
CHRISTENER, Wm. A. 16330.
CLARK, George 15304, 16479, Henry 15716, James 16108, William H. 15788.
CLEANER, Daniel 16384.
CLOMAN, James F. 16039.
CODER, John G. 16290.
CODY, John 16557.
COLBERT, Samuel 15792, 15793.
COLE, Jacob 15764, James 15387.
COLEMAN, George W. 16402, James H. 16277, John 16292.
COLLINS, George 15383, William H. 16397.
CONEY, William 15986.
CONRAD, Peter M. 15530.
CONSTANTINE, Richard 15497.
COOK, James 15315.
COOKSEY, Wm. 16341.
COOPER, John 15590, Thomas D. M. 15620, William T. 15697.
CORTRON, Harriet 15737, James 15737, Joseph 15753.
COTTMAN, Nathan 16541.
COUNCIL, Jacob D. 16046.
COX, Allen 16418, John 15679, Oliver 15554, William H. 15738.
CRAMBLETT, Joseph S. 15276.
CROCKER, Samuel G. 15998.
CROCKETT, Andrew J. 16131.
CRONAN, Daniel 16493.
CRONE, Jacob 16129.
CROSS, Michael 16004, Nicklos 15397, Susan 15622, Valentine 15622.
CROWTHER, Eli 15567, Samuel 15216.
CROWNER, James 16398.
CRUMP, John L. 16333.
CULLEN, James C. 15772.
CULLISON, George A. 15135.
CULVER, Charles B. 16140.
CUNNINGHAM, Aquilla 16237.
DAGEN, Frederick W. 16393.
DALLHON, Lewis 15985.
DANIELS, Jno. H. 15334.
DANNENFELSER, George 16128.
DANSBURY, Thomas 15944.
DARR, William 15580.
DAVIDSON, Edward 15350.
DAVIS, Archibald J. 15869, George N. 15991, Henry 15401, John 16347, Joseph 16545, 16546, Joshua 16495, Patrick 15842, Robert 15376.
DAY, Catherine J. 15297.
DeWATT, Lyman 16319.
DEAKINS, Sarah J. 15443.
DEAN, William E. 15324.
DEBRULER, James E. 16176.
DECKERD, Frederick J. 16220.
DECKMAN, Peter W. 16235.
DEFENDARFER, Solomon 15652.
DEVINNEY, Jeremiah 16301.
DEVOUGES, Victor P. 15481.

DEXTER, Samuel 16154.
DICKSON, James 16210.
DIETZ, Christopher 15969, John N. 16485.
DIFFENDERFER, Henry H. 15859.
DIFFEY, Victor 15313.
DILTY, William H. 16317.
DIRSCHNER, John C. 15690, 15691.
DITTMAN, John G. 16498.
DIXON, John F. 15261.
DOERR, Henry 15769.
DONNELLY, Patrick 15807.
DONOVAN, Patrick 15418.
DORSEY, Charles 16087, Frank 15505, George 15802, James 16415, James H. 15682, John 15825, 15829, 16329, Martin 15453, Robert 15486.
DOSCH, Andrew 16138.
DOTSON, Thomas 15966.
DOWDERS, John F. 16139.
DOWNEY, Sarah J. 16427, William F. 15157.
DOXZEN, Daniel M. 15949.
DOYLE, Hugh 16062, John 16437.
DRANE, David F. 16489.
DULTON, George F. 15863.
DUMER, August 16231.
DUNCAN, Charles Mason 16529, John F. 16422.
DUNNING, John 15925, Margaret A. 15925.
DUNPHY, Richard G. 15927.
DUVALL, Edmond B. 16331, George W. 16230.
DYSON, Wm. H. 16340.
EARLY, Harrison A. 15016.
EARNST, Carl 15373.
EATON, Lydia A. 15734.
EATON, Lydia A. 15734.
EBAUGH, Mary 15563, Nichola 15563.
ECCLESTON, James H. 16206.
ECKHART, William 16029.
EDIE, John E. 15669.
EDMONSTON, Thomas B. 15332.
EDWARDS, Amanda 16079, Catherine 16428, Chas. 16079, David 16132, Elizabeth 16133, Jarret 16338, John 16018.
EHRHARDT, George 16229.
EHRHART, Samuel 15599.
ELLINGSON, Julius 16227.
ELLISON, Geo. J. 15535.
EMMERICK, Ludwig 16336.
ENSOR, Charles 15606, Daniel E. 15436.
ERNST, Anton 16464, Regina 16464.
ESDON, William R. 16228.
EULAR, Jacob 15637.
EVANS, John C. 16224, Joseph T. 15270, Ogden 16078.
EXTINE, George 16236.
FADER, Chas. W. 16465.
FAIRFAX, Annie M. 15483.
FALCK, William C. 16164.
FAN, Jesse 15801.

FARLOW, David 15312.
FEAST, Mary J. 15250.
FISHER, Thomas A. 16242.
FISHPAW, William 15814.
FITZ, James L. 15748, Rebecca 15748.
FITZGERALD, John D. 15713, Margaret 15713.
FLANNIGAN, Patrick F. 15939.
FLEETWOOD, Wm. H. 15539.
FLORSTEDT, Frederick 15626.
FLYNN, Edward 16403, John 16156, Patrick 16326.
FOARD, Thomas 16058, William McK. 15672.
FOGARTY, Thomas 16433.
FOLEY, John 15514.
FOOT, William 15958.
FORD, Charles H. 16193, Francis 16021, John H. 16244, William G. 16267, William H. 15780.
FORDWELL, Sarah F. 15414, William A. 15414.
FORDYCE, J. N. 15823.
FORSTER, Henry 16366.
FORTUNE, Thomas 15523.
FOSTIE, Louis 16325.
FOUBLE, Oliver P. 15553.
FOUNTAIN, Stephen 16416.
FOWLER, Elizabeth 15761, James 15761.
FOX, George 16071.
FRANCIS, Nicholas 16487.
FRACTION, Othello 15982.
FRANK, George B. 15385.
FRANKLIN, Walter S. 15749.
FREASMAN, Joseph H. 15399.
FREDERICK Nelson 15686.
FREEBURGER, Columbus M. 16408.
FREELAND, Alfred 15668, Jacob 16533.
FRENCH, Oliver 15980.
FRITZ, George 15601.
FULLER, Wm. H. 16077, 16082.
FULTZ, George M. 15603.
FUNCK, David 16264.
FURRIER, Nathan G. C. 16449.
GALLION, Stansbury 15729.
GANELL, William H. 16383.
GARRISH, William H. 16282.
GARRISON, Alexander 16442.
GARTSIDE, John W. 15412.
GATCH, Thomas B. 16221.
GATHRIE, John A. 15635.
GAYLORD, John 15298.
GERE, Caroline 15598.
GERST, Jacob 16102, Katherine 16102.
GESFORD, John 16435.
GETTY, Andrew 15993.
GIBBS, Joseph 15661, William H. 16008.
GIBON, Howell 16324.
GIBSON, Andrew 16040, Howell 16324.
GILL, Joshua 15675.
GILLESPIE, John D. 16474, 16475.

GINNAMON, Samuel T. 15318.
GITTINGS, Isaac 15424, William 15876.
GLADMON, John W. 15946, 15947.
GOLDTHORPE, William 16476, 16477, 16478.
GOODWIN, John 15904, Wm. F. 15540.
GOODYEAR, Frederick 16306.
GORDON, James H. 15556, James R. 15658.
GORSUCH, Amelia 15765, John C. 15739, Thomas 15765, William 16060.
GOSNELL, George N. 16499, Mary J. 16110.
GOVER, Alfred 16535.
GRAHAM, John T. 15420.
GRANT, George W. 15921.
GREEN, Allen 15269, Catherine 16468, John 16364, John A. 15879, John W. 15768, Thomas 16203, 16273.
GREENBURY, Pearce 16050.
GREENE, Daniel 15299.
GREYS, Redmond 15909.
GRIFFIN, Matthew Luke 15460.
GRIMM, Daniel 15600, William 15562.
GRINE, Henry 15314.
GRIPP, Samuel 16346.
GROFF, Benjamin F. 15480.
GROSKAPF, George 16263.
GROSS, Ernest 16375, Thomas 16444.
GROVE, John W. 15532.
GRUBER, Henry 15820.
GURNS, William H. 15886.
GUTERMAN, Charles 15582, 15583, 15584, Victoria V. 15582, 15583, 15584.
HAGER, John C. 15565.
HAILE, Abraham 15609.
HAINES, Andrew 15777.
HALL, Albert G. 15331, Charles W. 16353, John 16037, Perry 15852, Susan 15471, William 16458.
HALLAM, William 16288.
HAMIL, Andrew T. 16388.
HAMILTON, Joseph A. 15389.
HAMMOND, Milbury 15901.
HANEY, Amos 16036.
HANNA, James R. 15485.
HANNAN, Francis C. 16492.
HANSON, Samuel 15751.
HARDEN, Nicholas 16542.
HARDER, Daniel 15356.
HARDING, William 16163.
HARE, Edwan 15862, Jesse 15552.
HARN, Edwin W. 15366.
HAROLD, Christopher W. 16511.
HARRIS, Asbury 16088, Henry C. 16064, 16065, John T. 16152, John W. 15680, Joshua L. 15671, Richard 15500,
HARRISON, Henry T. 16081.
HARTLEY, John R. 16248.
HARVEY, Caroline 16556, Harrison 16556, Philip 16436.
HATTON, George J. 16142.
HAUGHEY, Francis 15518, 15519.
HAUPT, William 16512.
HAWKINS, James 16016.
HAYWORTH, George 15370.
HEALY, James H. 15282.
HECKSCHER, Joseph N. 16481.
HEDGE, George 15888.
HEDGEMAN, Albert 16370, Henry 16202.
HEEWARA, John 15386.
HEIKEL, John 16256.
HEINZELMAN, Jno. 16460.
HELLEM, Isaac W. H. 15448.
HENRY, John 16158, Robert J. 15512, 15513, William P. 15868.
HENSON, Emily 15245, Jacob 15251, Mary 15251, Wm. H. 15245.
HERMAN, Emanuel 15952, 15953.
HERSEY, Joseph S. 15664.
HESLEY, Menie 16278.
HEUER, Frederick W. 16249.
HICKS, Benjamin 15902, John W. 15678.
HIGHLAND, George W. 16424,
HILDERBRANDT, Cheek 16297,
HILES, Edmond 15778,
HILL, Reuben 15569, William H. 16184.
HILTABRIDLE, Joseph 15978, Susan R. 15978.
HILTON, James 15303, Laura 15303.
HIMMER, Charles 16554, Teresa 16554.
HINES, Caleb B. 11866, Francis M. 15916.
HINKLE, 16318.
HINMAN, Charles A. 15020.
HINSON, Edward 11942, Theodore 12663.
HINTON, Daniel 15822.
HOAKER, Benjamin F. 15636.
HOBBS, William H. 16103.
HOFF, Joseph 15306.
HOFFMAN, Charles 16155, Cincinnatti 15571, Daniel 15779, Elizabeth 15571, Henry C. 15290, Peter B. 15623.
HOLBROOK, John H. 16134.
HOLLENSHADE, Thomas 16000.
HOLLEY, Elan L. 16312.
HOLLIDAY, Edward 15443.
HOLLINS, Richard 16001.
HOLMES, Elizabeth 15464.
HOLTER, William H. 16091.
HOLTZ, Edwin D. 15150.
HOOK, William 16216, 16217, 16218,
HOOVER, George 15557.
HOPKINS, Alfred T. 16174, Moses 16153, William F. 15673.
HORSEY, Howard 16542.
HOSE, Solomon 15275.
HOWARD, Benjamin 15771, Cornelias H. 15258, 15259,

Joshua 15903, William W. 15368.
HOWE, George 16186, William 14176, 16371, 16372, 16373.
HUBER, Antoine 16137.
HUDSON, Henry 15974.
HUGHES, Edward 16544.
HUMPHREY, John 15362.
HUMPHREYS, Edward 16287, Ralph 15984.
HUNT, George O. 15674, John W. 15613, Julia A. 15613, William T. 15503.
HUTTON, William H. H. 16469, 16470, 16471.
HYDE, Edward J. 16455.
IGLEHART, John H. 15272.
ILER, John W. 15742.
IRVING, William M. 16101.
JACKSON, Andrew 16354, John 16092, Jonas 16526, Thomas 16198.
JAMERSON, James H. 15754.
JAMES, Abel D. 15243, Jno. L. 16080, William H. 15867.
JANEY, E. W. 16265.
JANNEY, Thomas 15452.
JANNUSCH, William 16135.
JARRETT, James H. 15940.
JENKINS, William 16151, William T. 16124.
JETT, Mary A. 16243.
JOHN, David B. 16123.
JOHNSON, Anthony 15908, Bugauerie 15796, Frank 15941, Henry 16185, Hester A. 15941, James 15717, Jeff 16276, John 16170, 16490, John A. 16068, Joseph T. 15391, Samuel 16025, William 15372, William H. 15715, 16043, William J. 15971.
JOICE, Lewis C. 15797.
JONES, Aaron 15706, David 15883, Edward 15853, George W. 15326, Isaace 16548, J. Wymne 16252, James H. 15433, Louis C. 16316, Nathan W. 15349,
JORDAN, Stephen H. 16094.
JORDEN, Henry 16189.
JUBB, 8417, Lena 8417, Richard 16284.
KAHLER, Ellen J. 16225, William 16225.
KAISER, Charles 16482, Hannah 16482, John G. 16111.
KAKAFER, August 16395, Maggie 16395.
KALP, Henry 15607.
KANE, Andrew J. 16258, James 15834.
KAPP, Hosea 15957.
KEECH, James O. 15709.
KEENAN, Isaac 16551.
KEENE, Charles E. 15440.
KEENIE, Ezra 15377.
KEEPERS, Joseph 16528.
KELBAUGH, Thomas 15545.
KELLEY, Thomas F. 15813, William H. 15492.
KELLIM, Samuel A. 15885.
KELLY, Edward 16261, James 16335, Thomas F. 15827.
KELSO, George H. 15884, William 8984.
KEMP, J. McKendre 15494, 15495.

KERR, Robt. J. 16457.
KESTER, Jacob 16411.
KESTLER, Chas. J. 16337.
KEYES, Walter 16281.
KIDD, George 15841, Lloyd N. 15610.
KIDWELL, Charles W. 15325.
KING, Michael 15718, William 15860.
KIRK, Adam 15352, David 15617.
KITE, Daniel W. 15759, Henry C. 15291, John H. 15707.
KLENGSTEIN, Charles 16239.
KLINE, John 16114, Joseph 16027,
KNEUCKER, John 16420.
KNOTT, Edd A. 16075.
KNOWER, Edward C. 16510.
KNOWLING, John Henry 16523.
KONE, William H. 16015.
KOPPLEMAN, John H. 16226.
KREAMER, Christopher 16348.
KRODER, August 16461.
KROETZKAMP, Henry 16434.
KUHL, Leonard 16286.
KUMMER, Arnold 15266.
KURTZ, Henry 16169, Thomas 15798.
LAKE, Charles H. 15257.
LARKIN, Mary 16429.
LAVERN, William E. 16539.
LAW, John H. 16234.
LEAGUE, William F. 15714.
LEAHY, Rebecca C. 15865.
LEARD, Corbin 15752, Rebecca 15752.
LEATHERWOOD, Thomas 15300.
LEE, John H. 15319, William H. 16179.
LEMMEN, George 16051.
LENDAN, Henry 16524.
LENNING, John 16190.
LESCHINGER, Felix 16506.
LEWIS, Adelia 16438, Charles 15441, George A. 15564, Henry 16133, Jesse 15948, John W. 15945,
LIBBY, George W. 15365.
LIBEUS, Frederick William 15359.
LIGHT, Henry 16323.
LILLEY, George W. 15321.
LINDER, Edgar T. 15263, 15264.
LINDERMAN, Margaret 16483.
LINDIG, Elizabeth 16467, Ernest 16467.
LINZEY, James H. 15915.
LITZINGER, Richard 15992.
LIVINGSTON, LaRhett L. 16514.
LOFTUS, James 16307, John 16505.
LOGAN, Francis 16255, James J. 15287.
LOGUE, James T. 15534.
LOHR, Andrew 16085.
LOUDEN, William 16305.
LOUIS, Henry 16209, William 15983.
LOVEJOY, Perley R. 15406, Rebecca F. 15406.

LOWMAN, France T. 15305.
LOWE, John W. 15311.
LOWRIE, Alexander W. 16048.
LUBER, John 16459.
LUTZ, Charles G. 15363.
LYNCH, Ellen 16446, Jethro 15774.
LYONS, John R. 15887.
MacCLEMENTS, G. Peter 15641.
MacKENZIE, Hiram 15286.
MacLEA, Hester A. 15633, Wm. H. 15633.
McBUKOFFSKY, George H. 16124.
McCABE, John 15361.
McCANN, Mary C. 15588, Phinas J. 15588.
McCLEARY, Nelson 16298, Wesley 15594.
McCLELLAND, John T. 16211, Theodore 14665.
McCLENICK, Samuel 14462.
McCLINTOCK, Alexander 9003, Geo. 8374.
McCLURE, Jno. B. 8361.
McCLUSKEY, John 12569.
McCOMAS, John M. 16005, Mary A. 10559, Nancy 16005, Richard 11187, Robt. 10556, William 10559.
McCOMSEY, Mathias 15896.
McCOUBRAY, William R. 15648.
McCOWAN, James 16295.
McCOY, Johnny 15611, Mary L. 12513, William 11640, William H. 12513.
McCREA, Thomas 15194.
McCROSKY, James A. 16293.
McCULLEY, John H. 15431.
McDANIEL, James 16380, Mary B. 16380.
McFEE, Robert 16404.
McGLONE, Bernard F. 15828.
McINTOSH, David G. 15918, 15919.
McKENZIE, Annie V. 15310, David 16406, Jessie 15277.
McKETTRICK, Eliza A. 15294, Samuel 15294.
McKINZIE, Israel 15309.
McLAIN, Thomas 16313.
McMAN, John 16006, 16007.
McNEAL, Rachel B. 15732.
McSHERRY, Richard M. 15981.
MACK, Henry 15906, Mathias 16473.
MADDEN, Amos 15496.
MADDOX, John J. 16200, William E. 16197.
MAGEE, Benjamin 15592.
MAGLIDT, Henry 16073.
MAGNESS, Mosses N. 15327, Thomas M. 16240.
MAHONEY, John 16355.
MAKEL, Philips 16414.
MANGANO, Lazzara 15858.
MANNING, George O. 15864, John 12367.
MANNIS, Cecelia 16463, Emanuel 16463.
MARRIOTT, William H. 15357.
MARSHALL, John 16322.
MARTIN, Charles I. 15693, 15694, Eli 15703, Lewis 15470, William 16299.

MASEMORE, George H. 15700.
MASON, Ellen M. 15455, John T. 15455, Joseph 16488, Robert K. 15379.
MASSENBURG, Richard C. 15898.
MATHEWS, Benjamin 15959.
MAULFAIR, Amos C. 16308.
MAY, William 15180, William A. 15810.
MAYES, John 15684, John T. 15684, Nicholas 15685, Nicholas F. 15685.
MEADES, James 15951.
MEEK, Lucy L. 16003, 16004, Thomas 16003, 16004.
MERRYMAN, George 16304, Thomas H. 15733, W. H. 15712.
MERRYMEN, John W. 16052.
MEYER, Caroline 15631.
MEYERS, Alfred 15741, John 15631.
MICHAEL, Jacob O. 15615.
MICHAELS, Henry C. 16332, John 16369.
MILBURN, Thomas H. 16409.
MILLER, August 15283, Barbara 15280, Frederick 15897, George W. 15767, Henry 16098, John 16112, John B. 16251, John W. 15736, Joseph 15280, Joseph M. 16254, Thomas 16445, 16480, Walter B. 16362.
MILLS, Amanda 15468, Robert 16212.
MITCHELL, Alexander R. 15681, John W. 16501.
MOCK, Godfrey 15278, Margaret A. 15278.
MONROE, William 15585, 15586.
MONTGOMERY, Thomas 16314.
MOONEY, Jno. C. 15307.
MOORE, Catharine 15475, Henry W. 15475, Richard J. 16536, 16537.
MORFOOT, Robert 15766.
MORGAN, George W. 16127, John T. 16361, Thomas 15734.
MORIARTY, Matthew C. 15439.
MORLELER, Geo. H. 16357.
MORRING, Charles Robert 16042, Eliza A. 16043.
MORRIS, Dapprich 15880, William E. 16466.
MORRISON, James H. 15640, Thomas 15348.
MORROW, Hezekiah 15479, Isabella 16057, John 16056, Joseph 15476.
MUHL, Conrad 16342.
MULLEN, Patrick 15649.
MULLER, John 16120.
MURPHY, Josiah F. 15279.
MURRAY, Lewis 16023, Thomas 15954.
MYERS, Andrew 15284, Charles 16188, Clearfield 15520, Elisha 15561, Harry 16291.
MYRICK, John R. 16517.
NACE, Ferdinand 15994, Henry 15604, John 15549, Sarah A. 15604.
NAFE, Henry 15487.
NASGO, Charles 15833.
NASH, John W. 15854.
NEAL, John 15296.

NEBER, Mary V. 16396.
NEEL, John A. 15536.
NEHIER, John 16033.
NELSON, Daniel S. 15612, Samuel 15501.
NESS, Samuel R. 15506.
NEWKIRK, Joseph V. 16207.
NEWTON, Louisa 16374.
NICHOLS, Henry H. 15432.
NICOLL, William J. 15688, 15689.
NOLBERT, George 16180.
NOLLERT, Johanna 16180.
NORIS, Charles W. 15400.
NORRIS, James H. 16413, Richard S. 16238, Thomas 15746, Wm. 15537.
NORTON, Amisey A. 15369.
NORWOOD, Ebenezer 15333, Lambert S. 16107.
O'BRIAN, John 16496.
O'DELL, Daniel 16253, Sarah 16253.
O'KEEFE, Matthew 15938, Thomas 16012.
ONSSEN, James 16159.
OPINSHAW, Wesley W. 15655.
ORRELL, Edward B. 16334.
OWENS, Jerome B. 15322.
OWINGS, Joseph 16057, Samuel 16378.
PACE, Pleasant W. 15970.
PAFF, John J. 15644.
PARKER, Jacob 15806, James 15548.
PARKS, John A. 15910.
PARLETT, William J. 15866.
PARRISH, George T. 15330, John 15618, John H. 15320, Peter 15619.
PASTER, August 15293.
PASTERS, James T. 16187.
PATTERSON, Henry 15812.
PAUL, George W. 16145.
PAYNE, Henry O. 15973, Travers 16165.
PEAKER, William H. 16531, 16532.
PEARCE, Ephrin 15292, Louisa J. 15292.
PENDERGAST, James 16320.
PENNIMAN, Edward J. 15415.
PERKINS, James 15302.
PERRIE, Albert W. 15922.
PETTICORD, Joshua 15856.
PFEIFFER, George E. 15373.
PHENIS, Charles 16232.
PHILLIPS, George 15390.
PHIPPS, Alfred 15882.
PICKETT, William 15398.
PITCOCK, Charles H. 16104.
PITTS, Henry C. 16205.
POND, Erastus 15408, Mary B. 15408.
PORTER, Andrew 15285, Barbary 15240, George A. 16173, John 15240.
POTTER, Martha A. 16161,
POWELL, Bennett 15836, George W. 15805, Isaac 15745,

PRATT, Joseph 15928.
PRECHTEL, George 15566.
PREECE, Richard W. 16386.
PREGAL, Mathew 16041.
PRESLEY, John 15463, Mary 15463.
PRESTON, Alfred 15999, Henry 16201, Thomas 16204, Wesley 15428.
PRICE, Daniel 15760, Ephraim 15621, John S. 15705.
PROSSER, Charles S. 15735.
PURVIANCE, Daniel 15770.
QUEEN, Andrew 15375.
QUINN, Edward H. 15409, James 15546.
RAAB, George 16259.
RASP, John H. 16222.
RAYNER, John 16045.
RECKLER, Charles 15756.
REDING, John W. 16271.
REED, Andrew M. 15256, Annie J. 15426, Oliver C. 15967, William H. W. 15899.
REIF, Charles F. 15427.
REICHART, Philip 16084.
REILEY, Reuben 16367.
REMMEL, John H. 15458.
REMPEL, F. F. 15407.
RESSLER, Peter 15811.
REYNOLDS, Alfred D. 15381.
RHINAMON, David 15551.
RHODES, Thomas A. 16194.
RICHARDS, Henry S. 16266.
RICHARDSON, William H. 15639.
RIDENGER, John A. 16447.
RILEY, John L. 15750, Thomas 16401.
RIMMEY, Samuel M. 15341, William H. 15343.
RINGGOLD, Charles 15743.
RITELEY, Joseph 15338.
RITTER, Oliver R. 15410.
ROACHE, Jessie 15696, Lavina 15696.
ROAT, John 16191.
ROBECK, Charles 15790.
ROBERT, Henry 16521.
ROBINSON, Adam F. 15930, Chas. F. 16374, John 15791, John H. 15849.
ROBUST, John R. 15342.
RODGERS, Edward N. 15964.
ROGERS, William F. 15446.
ROHE, John 15763.
ROLLINS, Dorsey 15244.
ROSELIEP, John 15482.
ROSENBERGER, Louis 16223.
ROSENTHAL, Frederick 16115, Julius 16456.
ROSS, George H. 16247, Thomas 16399.
ROY, John 15763.
ROYSTON, Caleb 15572.
RUFF, Jacob F. 15456, John M. 15800, Mary R. 15800.
RUHL, Henry 15815, Sarah 15573, William 15573.
RYAN, Lauty 15843, William 15254.

RYE, Harry C. 15878.
RYNE, Hamilton 16243.
SAHERS, Mary E. 15447.
SANBLE, John S. 15550.
SANDS, Luther S. 16491.
SAUER, Charles C. 16126.
SAUMENIG, Henry 15394.
SAUTRE, Jacob F. 16166.
SCERER, John E. 16035.
SCHELLING, George B. 15979.
SCHENKEL, Leonard 16171.
SCHMIDT, George 16121, John 16146.
SCHMUCK, Henry 16167.
SCHOELKOPF, John 15799.
SCHRINER, John G. 16453
SCHROEDER, Augustus R. 16083.
SCHUARD, George 15353.
SCHULTZ, Amos 15692.
SCHUNCK, Robert 16279, 16280.
SCONNION, John Henry 16099, Sarah E. 16099.
SCOTT, Abraham 15789, Edward 15483, George W. 16283, Harry 15595, 15596, 15597, Jocuvus 16208, William I. 15688, 15689, William J. 16390, William S. 15662.
SEABOLD, George W. 16215.
SEAGER, George 16173.
SEALOVER, Asher 16257.
SEAS, Sanford E. 16538.
SEIF, Martin 16168.
SEIPP, George W. 15924.
SEITZ, Hyahtha C. 15667, Nicholas 15667.
SELLMAN, Jacob 15524.
SELMER, Charles 16516.
SENTS, Jeremiah 15329.
SHAEFFER, Joseph E. 15663.
SHAFFER, Francis 16047.
SHANNON, H. P. 15819, Henry P. 15832.
SHAW, John A. 16549, Silas H. 15704, William K. 16423.
SHEETS, Jacob 15950.
SHELDOLLAR, John 15242.
SHELTON, William H. 15628.
SHEPLER, George 16311.
SHERHOLT, Henry 15821.
SHIRLEY, William H. 15384.
SHOOK, Daniel J. 15473.
SHORT, Wm. H. 16350.
SHRAY, John F. 15482.
SHRIVER, Alexander 16294, Charles 9106.
SHUTLER, Charles 16377, William H. 16376.
SILVER, William J. 15308.
SIMMS, James W. 15654, Thomas 16192, Thomas A. 15670.
SIMS, George B. 16162.
SINGLETON, William H. 15782.
SKINNER, John B. 16177, 16178.

SKIPPER, George W. 16241.
SLADE, Abraham 15890.
SLENBAKER, John H. 15575.
SMALL, Levi H. 16381.
SMALLWOOD, Edward 15462, Nancy 15462.
SMALTZER, Martin 16053.
SMITH, Albert 16061, Amos 15913, Edward 15337, George 15490, George W. 15255, 15442, Henry A. 16144, Hugh B. 16505, Jacob 15660, James 15962, John 15450, 15824, 16460, John T. 16224, Larkin H. 16443, Peter 15423, 16275, 16289, Robert S. 15785, Thomas 15744, 16431, 16432.
SMITHSON, Hezekiah 15295.
SNARE, Adam 16095.
SNAVELY, Henry C. 16303.
SNYDER, John 16486, Labos 16315.
SOWDERS, Annie M. 16140.
SPANGLEY, Andrew 16157.
SPEAR, John C. 16430.
SPICER, John W. 15651.
SPURRIER, Edward 16527.
STABLER, Henry H. 15719.
STANFIELD, Thomas B. 15395.
STANSFIELD, Benjamin L. 15533.
STANTON, Edward 15817, John 16553.
STARKS, C. M. 15710.
STATEN, Jeremiah 16196.
STAUBER, George 16302.
STEINHAGEN, Richard 15850.
STEVENS, Alexander 15467.
STEVENSON, Elizabeth R. 15846, John M. 15846, William H. H. 15416.
STEWART, Charles W. 15757, Joel 15740, Wm. H. 16117.
STIER, George A. 15297.
STIFFLER, William H. 15698.
STIMAX, Isaac C. 15344.
STIMIX, Isaac C. 15374.
STINAGAN, John 15340.
STOCKSDON, Franklin 15777.
STREUBEL, Frank 16059.
STRICKLAND, William 15422.
STUMMER, William 16260.
SULLIVAN, George W. 15404, John 16472.
SUMWALT, William L. 13683.
SUPPLE, James 16525.
SUTTON, Gabriel 16339.
SWEETS, William H. 15310.
SWENE, Amon 15943.
TALBOTT, J. Fred. C. 15837, Jeremiah E. 15726.
TASCO, Samuel 16089.
TASE, Martin 15478.
TAWNEY, Andrew C. 15508.
TAYLOR, Benjamin F. 16086, Charles A. 16246, Harrison 16181, Isaac 15657, James 15614, James C. 15653, John H. 15773, Richard 16352, Robt.

Franklin 15838, Samuel 11498, 15934, Sarah E. 15773, Thomas 16328, Virginia E. 16181, William B. 15647, William J. 16213.
TEMPLE, Benjamin F. 16038, George W. 15345.
THOMAS, David N. 15727, George 16417, Gustus 15445, Jackson 16214, John 15521, John H. 15699, Richard 15851.
THOMPSON, George W. 16118, 16119, J. Richard 15629, Joseph F. 16419, Thomas 15687, William 16530.
THOMSON, Thomas 16172.
THORN, Charles A. 16136.
THRONGH, William 15784.
THURSTON, George A. 16513.
TIMMIS, Henry 15809, Sarah 15809.
TIMMONS, Charles T. 15929.
TODD, Samuel 15638.
TOLBERT, Samuel L. 15402.
TOMAY, Sylvester C. 15936.
TOMLINSON, Sarah E. 8878, William 8878.
TOMPHSON, Josiah 15914.
TOODLES, Richard 16090.
TRACEY, Elijah F. 16032, Thomas 15747.
TRACY, William 15795.
TRAINOR, Joseph 15488.
TRAPP, John A. 16028.
TRUEHEART, Adolphus H. 15271.
TRUSTY, Thomas W. 15413.
TUCKSON, Frederick 15758.
TULLY, 16157.
TURFORD, John 16451.
TURNBAUGH, John 16009.
TURNER, Edward 16522, Jas. H. 15840, John 15246.
UHLER, Johnzy 15803, William H. 15775.
UNDERWOOD, Elijah 16175, James 16122, Robt. 15238.
UNGER, Robt. B. 15248, Robt. D. 15234.
UPPERCO, Benjamin 15515.
UPTON, John W. 15360, Joshua M. 15364.
USEN, Isabella 15755, William 15755.
USSEN, George 15466, Jane B. 15466.
VANCE, James 16010, Martha J. 16010, William T. 15872.
VIRMILLION, Lorenzo 15396.
VOFEN, John 16063.
VOLLMER, John A. 16141.
WAGGONER, Henry E. 15527.
WAGNER, David 15355, Henry 15339.
WALES, Wm. R. 16502.
WALKER, John T. 15367.
WALLET, John 15555.
WALLIS, Jno. W. 15273.
WALLS, Charles 16300.
WALTEMEYER, Adam 15547.
WALTER, John W. 15474.
WALTJEN, Andrew S. 16250.
WAMSLEY, John S. 15438.
WARD, Felix 15917, Thomas 15968.
WARE, Joseph 16349, William H. 15323.
WARREN, John M. 16507.
WARRER, John N. 16394.
WATERS, Sarah E. 15289, Wm. H. 15289.
WATKINS, Benjamin 15247, Daniel R. 15875, Joseph 15484.
WATSON, Robert W. 16441.
WATTS, James H. 15387, Joseph W. 15235.
WEAVER, Daniel 15776, Lewis 16484.
WEBER, George 16309.
WEBSTER, John W. 16274.
WEDDLE, William J. 16387.
WEED, David M. 15434.
WEEKS, William 15911.
WEIMEISTER, Anna R. 15855.
WELCH, Benjamin 16345.
WELLS, Henry 15874.
WELSH, Daniel 15787.
WEST, Frank 16552, Henry 15382.
WEYHOMSER, Gerhart 16067.
WHARTON, George D. 16462.
WHEELER, John 15236, 15237.
WHITE, Michael H. 16410, Nathan 16272, William 15995.
WHITEFORD, John S. 16183.
WHITEN, William H. 15403.
WHITESEL, Charles 16547.
WHITTINGTON, Joseph 15988.
WHITTLE, Samuel N. 15923.
WIDDLE, John 16310.
WIEGER, William 15955, 15956.
WIGHTING, George 15830.
WILCOX, Elias 15844.
WILHELM, Daniel F. 15581, Emma 15845, Henry 15576, 15577, 15578, 15579, Joshua G. 15543, Samuel 15593, William T. 15587.
WILLIAMS, Alexander 16382, Andrew 16358, August 16150, Charles 16536, 16537, Charles J. 15725, Chas. H. 16385, Emma A. 16385, Frank 16522, Frederick 16097, George 15826, George W. 15976, Jacob 15783, James E. 15997, John 15656, Martha A. 16382, Resin 16368, S. Frank 16389, Sally E. 16389, William I. 15632.
WILLIS Lee 16321.
WILMOT, George H. 15328.
WILSON, Edward 15630, Edwin 15722, Gittings 16024, Turner 15873, William 15301, Willis 16321.
WINDER, Hicks 16022.
WINEHOLDT, George F. 15574.
WINGATE, Ambrose 16343.
WINKLER, Adam 16074.
WINSTANLEY, Mary E. 15999, William 15999.
WISE, Sarah 16439.
WISEMAN, George A. 10797, Grafton E. 15589, James

16500, John T. 9812, Mary C. 15589.
WOHLFAST, Elizabeth 16555, Harrison 16555.
WOLF, John 16113, John W. 15260.
WOLFE, John W. 16013.
WOLFENDEN, Thomas 15975.
WOODCOCK, Theodore W. 15417.
WOODS, Joseph E. 16055.
WOOTERS, Daniel 15881.
WORTHINGTON, Joseph 16520.
WRIGHT, John W. 15723, William S. 15509.
WYSHAM, William E. 15267.
WYATT, Lemuel C. 15645.
WYMAN, Joseph A. 16125.
YASTER, Charles M. 15871.
YATES, Lemuel A. 15421, Matthew 15419.
YELLOTT, John I. 15920.
YINGLING, William H. 15392.
YOUNG, Charles 15900, Geo. W. 15239, James 16379, John 16199, John T. 16014, Thomas H. 16011.
YOUNGER, Lemuel 15335, Richard 15347.
ZEIGLER, George 15358.
ZIEGLER, Francis 15665.
ZIEGMAN, William 15624.
ZIMMERMAN, William E. 15346.
ZWINK, John F. 16400.

www.ingramcontent.com/pod-product-compliance
Lightning Source LLC
Chambersburg PA
CBHW080437230426
43662CB00015B/2298